Sustainable Success with Stakeholders

'The business model of the pharmaceutical industry is on the test. In the future, only corporations will be successful who are able to implement the strategic management approach "Stakeholder View" in a visible and measurable way.'
**Dr Petra Danielsohn-Weil,** *CEO and President Pfizer AG, Switzerland*

'Communication is not just Orange's core business but also the most important prerequisite for a successful management. Since its foundation, Orange has greatly valued the constant dialogue with all its stakeholders and has therefore gladly agreed to participate in the case study of the authors Sachs, Rühli and Kern. The new book presents a profound analysis of how stakeholder dialogues are set up in firms and the impact which they have. The book contains valuable tips on how to establish and maintain a sustainable dialogue. Congratulations on this work!'
**Andreas S. Wetter,** *CEO Orange Switzerland*

'The sustainable success of Swiss Re's business is based on knowledge about its different stakeholder groups such as employees, customers, experts and other partners. Based on global activities in different cultural contexts, the strategic relevance of stakeholders will further increase for Swiss Re.'
**Charlotte A. Gubler,** *Member of the Executive Board, Swiss Re*

# Sustainable Success with Stakeholders

## The Untapped Potential

Sybille Sachs
Edwin Rühli
and
Isabelle Kern

First published 2009 by
PALGRAVE MACMILLAN

Palgrave Macmillan in the UK is an imprint of Macmillan Publishers Limited,
registered in England, company number 785998, of Houndmills, Basingstoke,
Hampshire RG21 6XS.

Palgrave Macmillan in the US is a division of St Martin's Press LLC,
175 Fifth Avenue, New York, NY 10010.

Palgrave Macmillan is the global academic imprint of the above companies
and has companies and representatives throughout the world.

Palgrave® and Macmillan® are registered trademarks in the United States,
the United Kingdom, Europe and other countries.

ISBN 978–0–230–22917–4

This book is printed on paper suitable for recycling and made from fully
managed and sustained forest sources. Logging, pulping and manufacturing
processes are expected to conform to the environmental regulations of the
country of origin.

A catalogue record for this book is available from the British Library.

A catalog record for this book is available from the Library of Congress.

10   9   8   7   6   5   4   3   2   1
18   17   16   15   14   13   12   11   10   09

Printed and bound in Great Britain by
CPI Antony Rowe, Chippenham and Eastbourne

# Contents

# List of Figures

# List of Tables

# Abbreviations

| | |
|---|---|
| ARPU | Average Revenue Per User |
| CBG | Coordination Against BAYER Hazards |
| CSR | Corporate Social Responsibility |
| CRM | Customer Relationship Management |
| EBITDA | Earnings Before Interest, Taxes, Depreciation and Amortization |
| EFQM | European Foundation for Quality Management |
| EIRO | European Industrial Relations Observatory |
| EITI | Extractive Industries Transparency Initiative |
| ESG | Environmental, Societal and Governance |
| GEO | Global Equity Organization |
| GPA | Group Public Affairs |
| HMO | Health Maintenance Organization |
| HRM | Human Resources Management |
| IFC | International Finance Corporation |
| IPCC | Intergovernmental Panel on Climate Change |
| ISS | Institutional Shareholder Services |
| MbO | Management by Objectives |
| MOSOP | Movement for the Survival of Ogoni People |
| NYSE | New York Stock Exchange |
| NGO | Non-governmental organization |
| OECD | Organisation for Economic Co-operation and Development |
| PRI | Principles for Responsible Investment |
| ROI | Return on Investment |
| SMS | Short Message Service |
| SRI | Socially Responsible Investing |
| TDC | Tele Danmark Communications |
| UNEP | United Nations Environment Programme |
| VHS | Video Home System |
| WMO | World Meteorological Organization |
| ZKB | Zürcher Kantonalbank (Zürich Cantonal Bank) |

# Acknowledgements

In writing this book several stakeholders have made substantial contributions. First of all, we would like to thank the University of Applied Sciences in Business Administration, Zürich (HWZ). We would particularly like to thank its principal, Professor Jacques Bischoff, who has always supported us financially and who always showed trust in and appreciation of our research. We are also grateful to Urs Marti, Delegate of the Board of Directors of HWZ, who has always supported us in our research projects.

A special thanks goes to Christine Luisi, who translated the German version of this book into English. She did it with great commitment, expert knowledge and patience when the authors introduced new phrasings that needed to be converted into proper English.

We are also grateful to Magi Wechsler, who succeeded in transforming a somewhat dry text into witty cartoons that summarize the contents of the chapters in a few pointed strokes.

We would also like to thank EABIS for supporting the publication of this book and for its cooperation during the past years.

All these stakeholder relations are proof of how fruitful and enriching the contribution of our stakeholders' knowledge and experience can be for value creation.

SYBILLE SACHS
EDWIN RÜHLI
ISABELLE KERN

# Foreword

Within EABIS (European Academy for Business in Society), stakeholders have always been identified as an important theme, both for the multinational companies and leading business schools in our network. As a result, in 2005, the Corporate Founding Partners of EABIS – IBM, Johnson & Johnson, Microsoft, Shell and Unilever – agreed to co-fund the HWZ-led project behind this book as one of their first priority initiatives.

As in many areas of corporate responsibility research, there is an acute need for projects that deliver practical results that managers can adopt in their daily work. Through their body of work around the Stakeholder View, Sybille Sachs, Edwin Rühli and colleagues have made a notable contribution to our understanding of the business case for excellence in stakeholder management.

The results of the extensive research done with seven Swiss firms – most of which are either global players themselves or are subsidiaries of global corporations – were initially presented at a 2007 conference in Zurich, but are further elaborated in this book.

Many firms confirm that stakeholders are important to them. But – as the book title, *Sustainable Success with Stakeholders: The Untapped Potential*, suggests – firms often lack a systematic approach to stakeholder management. They lack experience in defining their strategically important stakeholders, in engaging their stakeholders in value-creation initiatives, and particularly in understanding the potential benefit that stakeholders can bring to their own firm.

This book shows managers in a very hands-on manner how they can identify their stakeholders and cooperate with them in a way that is mutually successful and satisfying. The book includes numerous examples from the case studies and from international companies, illustrating the stepping-stones to a comprehensive stakeholder management framework.

This makes it an indispensable companion for managers of small as well as large firms. Moreover, it is also suited for business students who are interested in seeing how the theoretical concepts of the Stakeholder View can be applied in practice.

GILBERT LENSSEN
*President, EABIS*

# Introduction

We all know the catchphrases of today's management critics: short-term profit making, greedy managers, cold-blooded takeovers, scandals, cost pressure and layoffs dominate the discussion. A consequence of this are increased accusations against short-term profit thinking and market failures. Negligent boards of directors, arrogant managers, and indiscriminating advisers have plunged business as we know it into a crisis of confidence. Opinion polls in Europe and the USA show this, as for example the GfK Trust Index 2006 based on results in 19 countries. In this study, the most trustworthy persons are physicians and teachers while the least trustworthy are managers, journalists and politicians (see Figure I.1).

Bogle writes: 'CEOs are now close to the bottom of the barrel in public trust. One survey showed that while 75 percent of the general public trust shopkeepers, 73 percent trust the military, and 60 percent trust doctors, only 25 percent trust corporate executives – slightly above the 23 percent that trust used-car dealers.'[1]

Scandals result in not only loss of trust, but also enormous losses of wealth. The Enron stock, valued at $85 at the end of 2000, sank to 0 in the course of a year. The OECD calculated the loss of shareholder value at Enron to be over $9 billion. In addition to that over 6000 employees were laid off.[2]

At the same time, corporations are increasingly being challenged as to their function in society.[3] They are faced not only with economic competition but also with societal expectations, extending their responsibility. Stiglitz[4] claims in his recent book on globalization: 'One step in the right direction would be to have corporations take into account all stakeholders.'

Given this unpleasant situation, the challenge is to re-establish the credibility of corporations and managers with new comprehensive approaches, and most importantly to regain benefits for everyone involved. Reducing risk is one side of the coin; enhancing benefit, the other.

For many years, we have been engaged in the process of developing a new managerial approach. For this purpose we have analysed a large number of corporations and interviewed over 120 managers, all of whom are interested in establishing sustainable benefits for everyone affected by the actions and activities of corporations (cf. Appendix II). In this book, we want to show how corporations can be managed successfully and responsibly at the same time. We are presenting you, the reader, with some concrete examples and possible solutions. You are being addressed as a current or future business leader, or because you are interested in how the current crisis of confidence in business can be overcome. This management approach, which we call Stakeholder View, does not lend itself to only large corporations. Our research shows that valuable experience is also to be gained by small and middle-sized companies, since they are especially affected by the demands of their stakeholders.

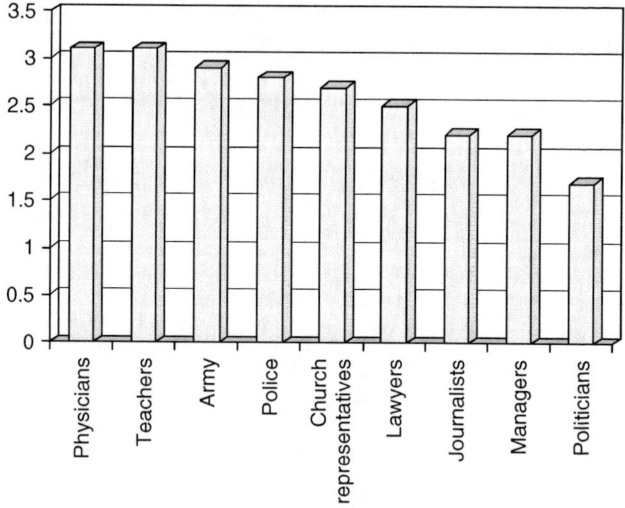


*Figure I.1*   GfK Trust Index (average value of trust of all respondents. Respondents could choose values from 1 to 4: 1 = high mistrust, 2 = some mistrust, 3 = some trust, 4 = high trust)
*Source*: Based on GfK (2006).

In the following chapters, we will see that those corporations, which have the support of different groups in performing their tasks, are successful, and that at the same time the groups profit too. These groups are the so-called stakeholders, and they include the shareholders or owners, customers, employees, etc. A corporation is successful when it succeeds in creating benefits for and with these stakeholders. It gains a comprehensive 'licence to manage' which – as we will demonstrate in detail – comprises three parts: the 'licence to innovate' thanks to a broad knowledge base; the 'licence to compete' because of a unique position in the field; and the 'licence to operate' due to the inclusion of the expectations of society.

At the end of the book, we include 'Take aways'. These are a brief summary of the perivous chapters and show you ways to implement stakeholder-oriented management. The 'Take aways' consist of ten principles and related questions that allow you to work through the principles.

We are inviting you to join us on a reconnaissance trip to find out how our corporations and companies can provide greater gains for us all in the future. The map of this trip is shown below:

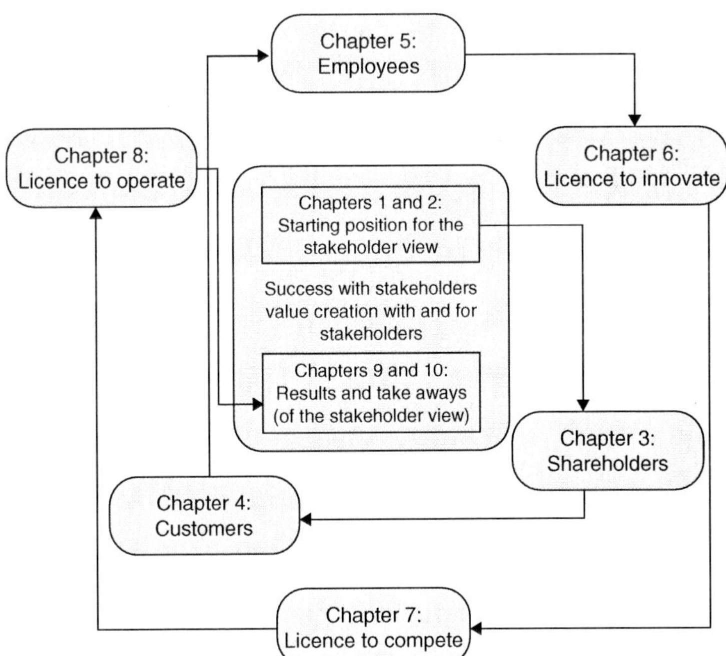

## Quick assessment of your corporations' stakeholder orientation

To start with we want to ask you to take the following test in order to clarify your stakeholder awareness.

## Instructions

Each of these questions is to be answered from the point of view of the corporation for which you are working. The scale is 1–10, with 10 being very high and 1 very low. At the end the numbers will be added together. The total corresponds to one of four types of stakeholder orientation (see Evaluation).

## Questions

1. How well do I know my firm's three most important stakeholders?

| 1 | 2 | 3 | 4 | 5 | 6 | 7 | 8 | 9 | 10 |
|---|---|---|---|---|---|---|---|---|---|
| Low | | | | | | | | | High |

2. How well can I justify why they are my most important ones?

| 1 | 2 | 3 | 4 | 5 | 6 | 7 | 8 | 9 | 10 |
|---|---|---|---|---|---|---|---|---|---|
| Low | | | | | | | | | High |

3. How often has my corporation contacted these stakeholder groups?

| 1 | 2 | 3 | 4 | 5 | 6 | 7 | 8 | 9 | 10 |
|---|---|---|---|---|---|---|---|---|---|
| Low | | | | | | | | | High |

4. How good is my contact to these stakeholder groups?

| 1 | 2 | 3 | 4 | 5 | 6 | 7 | 8 | 9 | 10 |
|---|---|---|---|---|---|---|---|---|---|
| Low | | | | | | | | | High |

5. To what extent has the contact with these stakeholder groups enhanced the innovativeness of my corporation?

| 1 | 2 | 3 | 4 | 5 | 6 | 7 | 8 | 9 | 10 |
|---|---|---|---|---|---|---|---|---|---|
| Low | | | | | | | | | High |

6. To what extent has the contact with these stakeholder groups enhanced the competitiveness of my corporation?

| 1 | 2 | 3 | 4 | 5 | 6 | 7 | 8 | 9 | 10 |
|---|---|---|---|---|---|---|---|---|---|
| Low | | | | | | | | | High |

7. To what extent is our corporation appreciated by these stakeholder groups as a valuable member of the society?

| 1 | 2 | 3 | 4 | 5 | 6 | 7 | 8 | 9 | 10 |
|---|---|---|---|---|---|---|---|---|---|
| Low | | | | | | | | | High |

8. To what extent can I justify that these stakeholder groups positively influence our strategic success?

| 1 | 2 | 3 | 4 | 5 | 6 | 7 | 8 | 9 | 10 |
|---|---|---|---|---|---|---|---|---|---|
| Low | | | | | | | | | High |

## Evaluation of your total

**Stakeholder guru (70–80):** You know the essentials of stakeholder management. We are convinced that your stakeholders appreciate working together with you as much as the other way around. When can we get to know you, in order to put you on our Best Practice list?

**Stakeholder initiate (50–69):** You know your stakeholders and also know how important their benefit potentials are for your corporation's success. Perhaps you can apply this knowledge even more systematically. We would be glad to help you in the process.

**Stakeholder freshman (17–49):** You have already decided to make a beginning at stakeholder management, but you lack the necessary know-how and the corresponding tools in order to successfully implement stakeholder management in your corporation. We are the experts you need.

**Stakeholder philistine (8–16):** Perhaps you like the idea, but you are probably missing a lot of stakeholder opportunities. Visit our website and get in touch with us, if you are interested in implementing this successful management approach in your corporation. There is a lot to do, but it is worth it.

## Your team of authors

*Sybille Sachs* has been Professor at the University of Zürich since 2003, and is Head of the Centre for Strategic Management: Stakeholder View at HWZ (University of Applied Sciences for Business Administration, Zürich). At the moment, she heads the research projects 'Good Practices of Stakeholder View' and 'ICT Supported Stakeholder Management as an Entrepreneurial Success Factor'. These projects are supported by a number of prominent national and international academic and research institutions. In addition to being a member of various national and international committees and boards of academic institutions, think-tanks and associations, Sybille Sachs is a founding member of the Forum Stakeholder View, whose goal is to strengthen the sustainable success of corporations through professionalizing their relationships to relevant stakeholders. She can be contacted at sybille.sachs@fhhwz.ch.

*Edwin Rühli* is Professor Emeritus for Business Administration at the University of Zürich. In 1970 he founded the Institute for Research in Business Administration there, which he headed until 2000. From 1984 to 1990 he was Pro-Rector of the University of Zürich. In the spring semester 1994, he was Guest Professor at Chazen Institute of International Management at the Business School of Columbia University in New York. He was and is a board member of various Swiss corporations. He is the author of the groundbreaking management books *Unternehmungsführung I–III* published in a number of editions. In the areas of international management, leadership, strategic management and stakeholder management, he has published more than 200 papers. He is President and founding member of the Forum Stakeholder View. He can be contacted at ruehli@isu.uzh.ch.

*Isabelle Kern* first studied English, German and History, and later Business IT. In between she spent a number of years in the multi-media field as author of programs for computer-based training. Currently she is a senior research assistant at the Centre for Strategic Management: Stakeholder View at HWZ (University of Applied Sciences for Business Administration Zürich), and wrote her dissertation at the University of Zürich on stakeholder and knowledge management. She can be contacted at isabelle.kern@fhhwz.ch.

An earlier version of this book was published in German under the title *Lizenz zum Managen. Mit Stakeholdern zum Erfolg: Herausforderungen und Good Practices* (Bern: Haupt, 2007). The current English publication was adapted and enhanced to an international version.

The cartoons in this book are by Magi Wechsler (Zürich), who succeeded in enriching a somewhat scientific text with witty graphical interpretations.

## Notes

1  Bogle (2005), p. 22.
2  Von Frentz (2003); OECD (2002); Citizen Works (2002).
3  Sachs (2000).
4  Stiglitz (2006), p. 203.

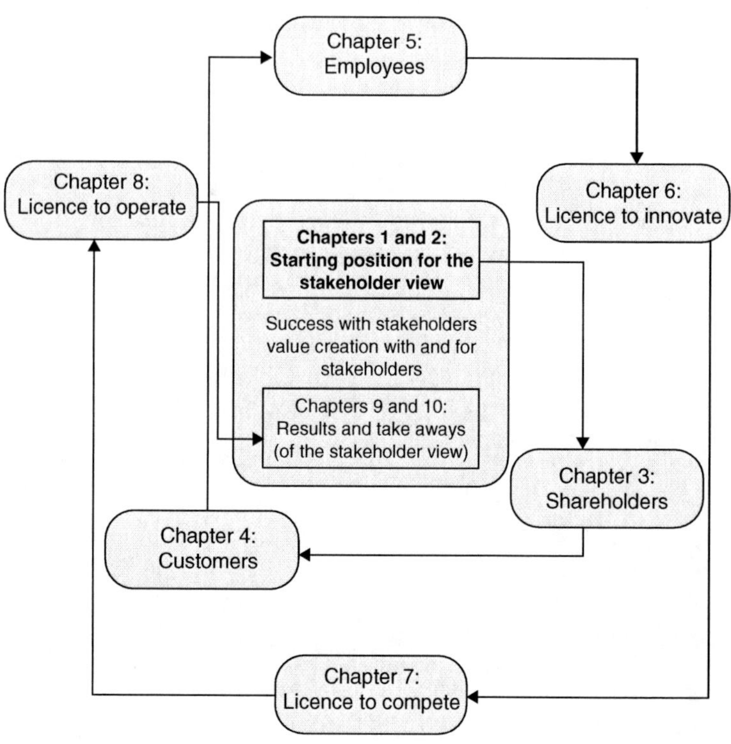

Chapter 5:
Employees
Chapter 6:
Licence to innovate
Chapter 8:
Licence to operate
Chapters 1 and 2:
Starting position for the
stakeholder view
Success with stakeholders
value creation with and for
stakeholders
Chapters 9 and 10:
Results and take aways
(of the stakeholder view)
Chapter 3:
Shareholders
Chapter 4:
Customers
Chapter 7:
Licence to compete

# 1
# Why put all your eggs in only one basket?

Imagine you are organizing a concert. In doing so, you need the help of different people or groups. As the event organizer you may be convinced that the success of the concert depends only on finding strong financial sponsors. Some of your colleagues may disagree saying that the success depends on the musicians. Others may say that the best musicians mean nothing if one is unable to attract the right audience.

No doubt all of them are right. Is it not true that various actors are needed in order to succeed in any enterprise, whether it be family, politics or science? And business, including your corporation, is hardly an exception.

In the following case, we can see how the collaboration of different people interested in the same issue led to an astonishing success.

> **Example: Climate Report**
> When the World Meteorological Organization (WMO) and the United Nations Environment Program (UNEP) realized that global climate change could become a problem, together in 1988 they founded the Intergovernmental Panel on Climate Change (IPCC). The IPCC describes its role and activities as follows: 'The role of the IPCC is to assess on a comprehensive, objective, open and transparent basis the scientific, technical and socio-economic information relevant to understanding the scientific basis of risk of human-induced climate change, its potential impacts and options for adaptation and mitigation. The IPCC does not carry out research nor does it

monitor climate-related data or other relevant parameters.
It bases its assessment mainly on peer-reviewed and published
scientific/technical literature.' Approximately 2500 scientists
as well as representatives of over 100 countries belong to the
IPCC. In order to document climate change, the IPCC has
established three international working groups and one task
force with the following duties:

- 'Working Group I assesses the scientific aspects of the climate system and climate change.
- Working Group II assesses the vulnerability of socio-economic and natural systems to climate change, negative and positive consequences of climate change, and options for adapting to it.
- Working Group III assesses options for limiting greenhouse gas emissions and otherwise mitigating climate change.
- The Task Force on National Greenhouse Gas Inventories is responsible for the IPCC National Greenhouse Gas Inventories Programme.'

These working groups published their fourth Assessment
Report on climate change in 2007, which received a great deal
of attention internationally. Scientists from all over the world
contributed. For their comprehensive work, the IPCC together
with former US Vice President Al Gore received the Nobel
Peace Prize in 2007.[1]

## An appeal for a comprehensive view of management

In this book we have set ourselves the goal of showing the possibilities
of how you can increase the chances of success for your corporation
and your projects by systematically using the potential of strategic
stakeholders. The essence of the appeal is that things work out better
when done together with various partners than when done alone.
Cooperation with several interested partners is superior to going solo.
Given the intensity of competition, it is time to consider how the
usefulness of potential of stakeholders in various areas of strategic
management can be implemented in practice.

Perhaps you are asking yourself: what are stakeholders? Am I a stakeholder? When we speak about stakeholders, we mean the following:

**Stakeholders are persons or groups of people who contribute to the wealth-creating activities of a corporation. Stakeholders either receive or provide benefits or bear or provide risks.**

Some of the different stakeholder functions can be illustrated in the daily life of Mrs Smith. She is married and the mother of two children, and she works in a bank. She is a member of the clerical staff of the bank, and as an employee she is a stakeholder of the bank. She was trained and has specialized in the consolidating procedures of big banks; as a result she has a specific investment in the corporation. For the corporation, her qualifications are important value creation. However, she will be able to apply her knowledge only in a similar job, and this gives her qualifications a somewhat limited market value. If she were to lose her job and not be able to find another one with the same requirements at another big bank, she would have invested a lot of time in training and getting experience for nothing. She therefore carries a firm-specific risk. On the other hand, the big bank depends on employees like Mrs Smith developing their knowledge and making it available. Without Mrs Smith's knowledge and commitment, the bank would not operate as efficiently.

Mrs Smith has bought a racket for her daughter which is a new development that has just come onto the market. After a short while, the racket has to be repaired and after work, at the sports store where she is picking it up, the salesperson wants to know how her daughter likes the new racket. As a customer of the sports store, in responding to such a query, Mrs Smith is making her experience available so the store can use it when buying new rackets for future stocks. The store is benefiting from customer experience. In turn, Mrs Smith's daughter will benefit later on from further improved tennis rackets.

In the evening in a town near the airport, Mrs Smith as a member of the interest group 'Quiet Neighbourhoods' meets with the management of the nearby airport. She is now in the role of stakeholder expressing societal expectations towards a corporation. Her children suffer from the flight noise. Airport operations cause them to bear a health hazard. If no agreement can be reached, the airport runs the risk that the interest group will carry out its threat to stage a protest demonstration in the entrance hall of the airport. This would cause passenger flights to be delayed. The interest group, and Mrs Smith with it, would thereby become a liability for the airport.

The example can be expanded indefinitely. What is clear in any case is that we are all part of a web of stakeholder relationships.

Three things are important for our understanding of the meaning of stakeholders:

1. **We are all stakeholders in different situations and functions. Thereby we bear or provide risks, and receive or create benefits.**
2. **Corporations are exposed to the expectations of their stakeholders, as well as to their risk and benefit potentials.**
3. **Corporations are stakeholder-oriented when they systematically consider the risk and benefit potentials of their stakeholder network in their strategic behaviour.**

## The early birds in stakeholder thinking

What does stakeholder thinking mean for you and your corporation? In our empirical investigations, we discovered that more and more managers are realizing that a narrow focus on the shareholders alone is insufficient for meeting current demands. In a recent study conducted by McKinsey in which some 400 CEOs were interviewed, 'over 90% stated that their corporations were doing more than they had five years ago to include environmental, societal and governance (ESG) considerations in their core strategy.'[2]

Decisive events or fundamental changes in their own corporations or fields have made corporations increasingly sensitive to the concerns and potentials of a whole range of stakeholders. More than 30 years ago some European and Japanese corporations were already intentionally behaving in a stakeholder-oriented manner, as the following examples show:

> **Example: Volvo (Swedish car manufacturer)**
> At the beginning of the 1970s, car manufacturers saw themselves confronted with the following problem: work on assembly-lines was repetitive and dull; the workers were consequently unmotivated and dissatisfied. The result was absenteeism, high fluctuation and a significant number of people who no longer wanted to work in the car industry. Volvo was also confronted with this problem, and responded with an entirely new solution: the workers received more rights and responsibilities, and as recognized stakeholders they were given a voice in determining the work procedures.

The Volvo model included the following points:

- A process of job rotation enabled the workers to develop new abilities and a better understanding of the work of their colleagues.
- The workers received a financial share of the production profits.[3]

Volvo was very successful with its intentional stakeholder orientation. Not only did the fluctuations and dissatisfaction of the workers decrease, but at the same time productivity increased. By the end of the 1980s, General Motors had adopted parts of the Volvo model in its own plants.

**Example: JVC (Victor Corporation of Japan, Japanese producer of electronics and software)**

At the beginning of the 1970s, the two corporations Sony and JVC were competing with each other in developing the video cassette. The market leader Sony gradually lost its position to JVC. The reason was that JVC was willing to work together with other corporations and to give them a say in refining the video system standards (the so-called VHS, Video Home System). This included lengthening the two-hour recording time. In addition, JVC provided its partners with support in production and marketing. JVC also cultivated a very different style from Sony: JVC was friendly when dealing with its partners; it was open towards them and interested not only in developing the joint standard for video cassettes but also the video recorder. This led to the potential production partners becoming convinced that JVC wanted to develop the recorder with them. Sony, on the other hand, tried to develop and establish a standard called Beta on its own. The result was that their system practically disappeared from the market.[4]

In these examples, cooperation with stakeholders clearly had a positive effect on the corporation.

## The era of shareholder value fanatics

As the international financial market became more professional and influenced by US economic thinking, more and more corporations worldwide including those in Europe began to orient themselves increasingly to shareholder value. The primary consideration of many managers became how to enhance contributions to the shareholders. This may have led to revising some antiquated structures, but it also led to a more narrow view. What were the long-term effects? The following example shows a possible negative effect of shareholder-value thinking.

> **Examples: Danone (French food group) and Marks & Spencer (British department store chain)**
> In 2001 Danone and Marks & Spencer announced cutbacks in employment. Danone did this as a 'precautionary measure', despite making a good profit at the time. Marks & Spencer attempted to overcome its crisis by restructuring. Both corporations explained their measures with the same reasoning: in order to remain competitive in a global economy and to increase profitability for the shareholders, they were forced to cut back employment. The increased shareholder orientation came at the expense of other stakeholders.[5]

Despite these two examples, there are enormous differences, also within the European Union for example, in the extent to which corporations are oriented to shareholder value. This is shown in an EIRO study (European Industrial Relations Observatory) from 2002.[6] Interestingly, there is a connection between shareholder thinking and the legal rights granted to employees during corporation restructuring. For example, in Britain and Ireland employees have few rights. By contrast, social partnership in Austria, Denmark and Luxembourg is traditionally strong and so far shareholder-value thinking has only minor influence. The position of Sweden, Belgium and Germany is more in the middle, where shareholder-value thinking is promoted by the internationalization of big corporations, but at the same time is held in check by social partnership.

## Stakeholder management – a new horizon

How is the situation today? For more than ten years, our research team has been investigating the extent to which different corporations are successful, when they include the benefit and risk potentials of their strategic stakeholders in their value-creating processes. In doing so, we have set ourselves the goal of working out the criteria of Good Practice, and of portraying corporations which have learned intentionally and professionally to draw on the benefits of their stakeholder relationships. We have found persuasive examples based on the considerations that underlie this book. You will find a description of our research project as well as a list of our most recent conference papers in Appendix I: Research Project 'Good Practices of Stakeholder View' (p. 173).

## Triggers for a stakeholder orientation

In the corporations we investigated we could see that there are primarily three catalysts for learning processes that lead to stakeholder-oriented thinking and acting:

1. **Wake-up calls**
2. **Outside pressure**
3. **Core values**

### After the wake-up call nothing is as it was

One possible reason for a learning process to take place in stakeholder management is a wake-up call. After being shaken up, as a rule corporations not only change the direction of their strategic management, but also, in particular, their corporate culture and stakeholder relationships. They go through what is called a transformational learning process.

Natural phenomena can be wake-up calls. Hurricane Andrew in 1992 was a wake-up call for the insurance business. In addition, in the years 1992–94, there was a culmination of catastrophes. This was and still is the reason why Swiss Re, the world's largest reinsurer, is making studies of whether those catastrophes were merely aberrations in standard deviations or whether they represent a trend. These analyses are assisted by the growing recognition of climate change.

As a result, Swiss Re has engaged itself strongly in different working groups and platforms in order to discuss how climate change influences natural catastrophes. In doing so, it has also sought contact with those NGOs (non-governmental organizations) which appear to be competent stakeholders in the matter.

An impetus in the learning process in stakeholder management can also be a fundamental change in the general regulatory conditions. This was the case in the 1990s in many European countries including Switzerland. The liberalization of the market in the telecommunications sector was a wake-up call for the former monopolist Swisscom, which was partially privatized as a result. Due to decades of a close relationship to 'country and people', the corporation was strongly anchored in a large stakeholder network and a broad stakeholder orientation has remained since this time. However since the partial privatization, Swisscom has had to work out an entirely different role in dealing with former stakeholders (government, administration, labour unions, politics). The Federal government has shifted from being purely the chief administrative authority to becoming a (major) shareholder. There are also new stakeholders like external shareholders and representatives of financial markets. In addition, the mobile telephone and Internet boom have changed the relationship with customers, who previously did not have a real choice. All this has fundamentally changed the strategy and the corporate culture of Swisscom, as emphasized by an interview partner:

> 'As a state monopoly enterprise, the various stakeholders were hardly a topic for us; instead it was primarily the Federal government, as the chief administrative authority. And then suddenly after the liberalization, all the stakeholders became important. … The realization that other stakeholders are important was not effective until after the liberalization, when one suddenly realized that one was no longer in a protected operating framework. The corporation image became an important issue; before it had played a subordinate role.'

The catalysts for dramatic changes can also be situations that the corporation has basically misjudged. Let us look again at the telecommunications industry in Switzerland. After a phase of hyper-growth and almost unlimited possibilities, the sudden, and for market members unexpected, stagnation in growth at the end of 2002 and beginning of 2003 resulted in forced downsizing, restructuring and cost-cutting. Orange Switzerland, the national subsidiary of the International Orange Group, was forced to close down a whole call-centre. At the same time the owners raised pressure to succeed, so that fundamental changes were unavoidable. On the one hand, the information policy was unfortunate; and on the other, management assumed that the personnel would simply accept the sudden change in values and such consequences as relocation. However, they completely misjudged the willingness of the employees to change location. First, the employees mobilized the union as a new stakeholder for their concern. Then there were strikes, a polemical media campaign, and tension and disputes with the employee organizations. Orange Switzerland had to learn to deal with situations, and even more with stakeholders, they had hardly noticed before. All of a sudden the employees as negotiating partners, the unions, the media and the public were of strategic importance. As an interview partner stated:

> 'The phase of building up the corporation had been a hype. The only thing anyone was interested in was growth, growth, growth. Then suddenly we realized that we had to adapt our structures, and that had consequences for 100 employees. All those things triggered a lot of learning. Now before spending any money to build something up, one asks oneself five times whether it will be a success in the long run. Those are things we had to learn the hard way.'

In this corporation, what happened resulted in a completely new way of dealing with stakeholders such as the employees, media and social partners.

### Business partners rock the boat

Learning processes are not always as dramatic as wake-up calls. Corporations often become more stakeholder-oriented because of the changing expectations of direct business partners, customers, suppliers or investors. For example, in one of the corporations we investigated, supply contracts are awarded not only on the basis of market criteria but also on the basis of sustainability. As selective criteria, the relationship of potential suppliers with their stakeholders can also be taken into consideration. In this way, the corporation can exert pressure on its suppliers regarding their sustainable stakeholder orientation.

After years of developing quietly, the pharmaceutical industry is beginning to get panicky. For many years, it seemed as though high prices and above-average profits were as good as guaranteed for all health product providers. However, recently the pharmaceutical corporations are being confronted increasingly with demands and challenges from their stakeholders. The attack of many stakeholders is directed at the problem of the rising cost of health care. On the other hand, the rising cost of innovations, the improved quality of services, and changes in demand based on structural demographic change are less often mentioned.

In this context, the pharmaceutical corporations are generally being challenged to bring about a fundamental change in their business model, in the form of a comprehensive stakeholder management approach. An interview partner at Pfizer had this to say:

> 'It's a multiple problem. To put it bluntly, Big Pharma is a gigantic, impersonal profit machine which generates its profit at the expense of patients with exaggerated prices for drugs and which keep physicians docile with generous donations so they sell their drugs. And of course all at the expense of patients which means at our expense in the end, at the expense of a social health care system. This perception is of course totally unfair. And the media play a decisive role in shaping this perception.'

It is typical of this form of learning process that, on the basis of the changes in the stakeholder situation, often strategic orientation also has to be adapted.

---

**Example: Nike (US manufacturer of sports goods)**
For years, Nike was strongly criticized for having its sports goods manufactured in sweatshops. The workers producing Nike clothes and shoes earned too little to live on. They were prohibited from unionizing, and they were exposed to health and safety hazards while at work. In 2005, the critics of Nike celebrated a breakthrough: the corporation published a

'Corporate Responsibility Report' for the first time in its existence. The report acknowledged the deplorable conditions in the supplier corporations, for which the corporation had been denounced. At the same time, it published the names and locations of over 700 supplier corporations. For the last 10 years the activists had been demanding this, so that the conditions in the factories could be inspected by independent reviewers. Since then Nike annually publishes an extensive Corporate Responsibility Report. In addition, on its homepage Nike writes: 'We see corporate responsibility as a catalyst for growth and innovation, an integral part of how we can use the power of our brand, the energy and passion of our people, and the scale of our business to create meaningful change.' In 2006 this led to Nike being ranked 13 (the previous year Nike was 31) in *Business Ethics Magazine*'s annual '100 Best Corporate Citizens'. In compiling the ranking, *Business Ethics Magazine* considers criteria such as corporate governance, diversity, employee relations, and human rights.[7]

**Stakeholder traditionalists**

There are also corporations that have been stakeholder-oriented since their founding. The cases we have met thus far are almost exclusively family corporations, or corporations with a public service mandate.

The founding family often represents specific core values. In the case of Trisa, an international provider of tooth care products, these values concern its employees. Due to the beliefs of the founding family, in 1970 Trisa introduced the idea of employees being shareholders, and the board of directors consisting in equal part of family members and employees.

Corporations founded in the public interest often have the duty of advancing the welfare of certain stakeholder groups, which are part of the public service mandate given to them by the state. For example: the 1981 Swiss Federal law on accident insurance assigned Suva the rights to offer accident insurance in the areas of construction, manufacturing, transportation and civil service, in a monopolistic context but also in a stakeholder-oriented way. At the beginning of the twentieth century, there had been a provision gap which the Suva mandate closed. Today Suva provides comprehensive coverage with great success in the areas of prevention, insurance and rehabilitation.

Corporations with traditional stakeholder-friendly core values tend to change their stakeholder orientation in smaller steps. In doing so, they seldom make basic changes in their strategy or core values. For these corporations, stakeholder-oriented learning is already part of the way they operate.

Looking at stakeholder relationships of corporations from a historic perspective, one can see that the stakeholder orientation these corporations have today is sometimes the result of many learning steps and different learning types: fundamental learning processes brought on by wake-up calls alternate with small learning steps on the basis of a distinct stakeholder orientation.

As an example, we have been able to identify nine important learning steps in the development of Swiss Re since 1863. These were catalysed by important internal or external events that changed and even today shape the strategic, structural and cultural development of the corporation, specifically also its stakeholder relations. The expression 'history matters' is also true for stakeholder relationships; the 'footprints' of history are often clearly recognizable in the current behaviour of a corporation. Table 1.1 below lists examples showing the nine learning steps of Swiss Re.

From the beginning, Swiss Re has been strongly employee oriented. In addition to its employees, the corporation has successively drawn customers, shareholders, regulators and NGOs into its strategic considerations as a result of the events mentioned above. Each of

*Table 1.1*   The nine learning steps of Swiss Re

| | |
|---|---|
| Event 1: Wake-up call<br>  Mid 1800s | Fire catastrophes (i.e. Hamburg 1842) |
| Event 2: After 1870 | Second Industrial Revolution |
| Event 3: Begin. 1900s | Catastrophes of previously unknown dimensions (San Francisco earthquake 1901; *Titanic* 1912; World War I) |
| Event 4: 1930s | Stock Market Crash, world wide economic crisis |
| Event 5: After 1945 | Unprecedented economic growth and technological progress |
| Event 6: End of<br>  20th century | Series of natural catastrophes |
| Event 7: Since 1990 | Globalization, world as "global village" |
| Event 8: After 2000 | Economic down-turn and corporation scandals |
| Event 9: 11.9.2001 | Terrorism |

these events contributed to the continuous development of Swiss Re's stakeholder relationships.

Such learning steps confirm another expression, namely 'path dependency'. Each step on the way of development in stakeholder relationships is influenced by previous learning processes. Even in radical transformation, such as Swisscom had to go through in the course of liberalizing and partially privatizing the telecom industry in Switzerland, the forces of the past are at work. Even though exposed to competition, Swisscom is still regarded by many stakeholder groups as a national utility. As a result, its strategy is strongly influenced by regulations and political pressure.

These examples show how essential it is for your corporation to know about past developments and to draw them into current strategic considerations.

The first chapter can be summarized by the following motto:

**Stakeholder management is strategically relevant. Earlier experience with stakeholders influences how we deal with them today; history matters.**

The following questions are relevant for your consideration:

1. What kinds of events in the history of my corporation are important for future stakeholder relationships?
2. What and how have my corporation and I learned from them?
3. Are there core values in my corporation which could further a stakeholder orientation?
4. How well is the awareness of the meaning of stakeholders developed in my corporation? Where is my corporation on the following scale?

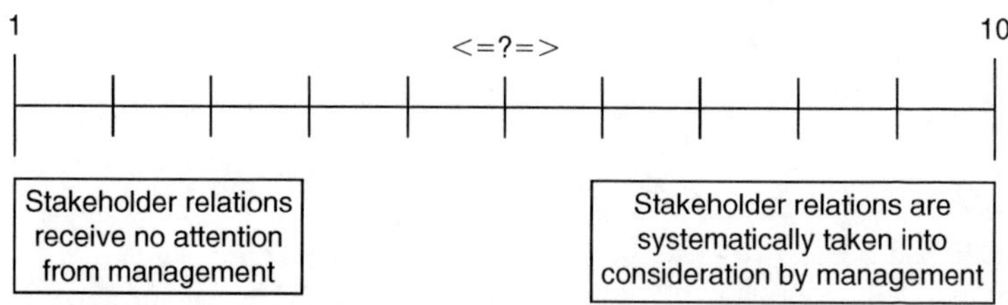


*Figure 1.1*   Appraisal of stakeholder awareness in your corporation

## Notes

1  IPCC (2007).
2  Waddock *et al.* (2007).
3  Gibson (1973); Gyllenhammar (1973); Hauck and Ross (1988).
4  Cusumano *et al.* (1992).
5  EIRO (2001b, 2001c).
6  EIRO (2002).
7  Global Exchange (2007); EFJ (2004); Nike (2007); Raths (2006).

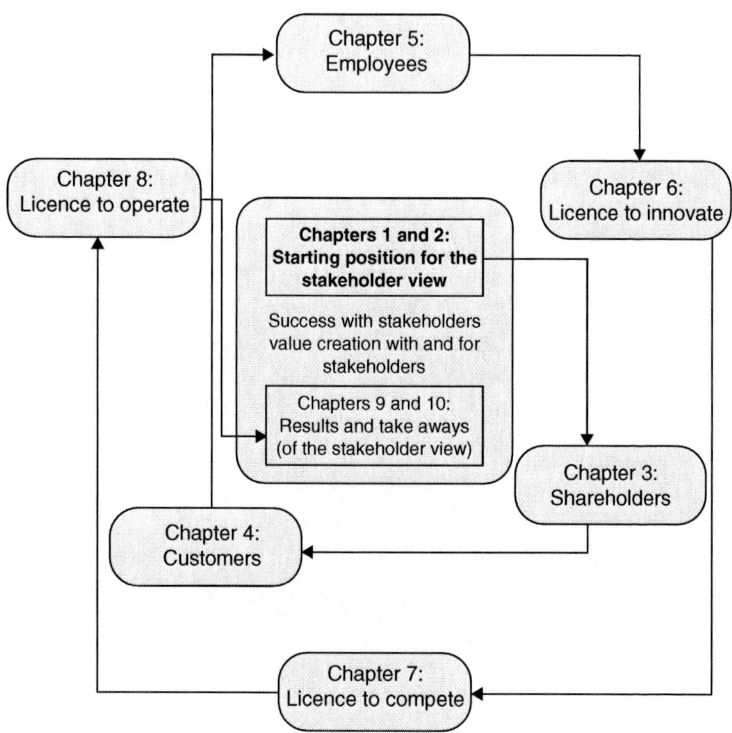

Chapter 5:
Employees
Chapter 8:
Licence to operate
Chapter 6:
Licence to innovate
Chapters 1 and 2:
Starting position for the
stakeholder view
Success with stakeholders
value creation with and for
stakeholders
Chapters 9 and 10:
Results and take aways
(of the stakeholder view)
Chapter 3:
Shareholders
Chapter 4:
Customers
Chapter 7:
Licence to compete

# 2
# Who are my fellow stakeholders?

Many corporations think they know who their strategically relevant stakeholders are. In our studies, we found that this opinion has often come about accidentally without the benefit of systematic thinking. This chapter demonstrates why professional stakeholder mapping needs to be seen as being as essential as budgeting, since both managerial tools aim to allocate and disseminate resources efficiently. The follow-up question is who the most important stakeholders are. One is particularly interested to know whether and to what extent they could be useful or harmful.

## Shareholders are everything

In one of our interviews, a manager reflected on the priority of different stakeholders, and asked himself the question of what motivates him to get up every morning to go to the office:

> 'Do I get up to make my employees happy? Certainly not. We are not a charity organization. Or it is to satisfy my customers? Satisfaction is not enough, if the figures don't add up. In the end, I am obliged to the shareholders since they provide the capital. Above all, I have to pursue their interests, because they are bearing a corporation risk.'

One can see it this way; though most managers would probably prefer a cup of coffee over the importance of the shareholders to make them feel ready and raring to go in the morning. In fact our studies also show that the preferential position of shareholders in corporations is widely shared. Here is a typical quote from one of our case studies:

> 'I think the shareholder has to be the most important stakeholder. We get our capital from our shareholders. There is of course the classic triangle among shareholders, employees and customers. Certainly one has to look after the customers. And if the employees are happy, then in the end the shareholders are too. However, our most important obligation is to fulfil the expectations of the shareholders. I believe that in the Anglo-Saxon world the original magic of the triangle is losing its meaning. The Anglo-Saxons are very much oriented to the shareholders, while the non-Anglo-Saxons are more focused on the customers and employees.'

## The grand design model

Where does this concentration on the interests of the shareholders come from? In business economics, one calls this orientation the 'grand design model'. It focuses on the owner–management relationship. This orientation developed historically in the twentieth century with an increasing separation of ownership and management, which as time went on led to some fundamental problems. On the basis of the gap between ownership and management, divergent interests developed. The current discussion with the catchphrase 'corporate governance' demonstrates this nicely. We shall come to this subject in the next chapter, when we look at the role and position of shareholders from a stakeholder perspective.

Since the financial commitment of the ownership of the corporation is central in this kind of economic thinking, it is also known as the financial model of the corporation. The financial model still dominates the literature on business economics, as well as the decision making in corporations. It clearly has a preferential position: the shareholders make their capital available so that the corporation can do business. They make firm-specific investments. The management of the corporation uses this capital for corporation purposes, and receives remuneration for doing so. The shareholders potentially bear the risk that management might, unintentionally or out of personal interest, mismanage the capital or even lose it. In other words, the ultimate responsibility of management in this financial model is to use the capital in such a way as to make a profit for the shareholder. Milton Friedman, the well-known economist and Nobel prize winner, also emphasizes this responsibility in his book *Capitalism and Freedom*:

> Few trends could so thoroughly undermine the very foundations of our free society as the acceptance by corporate officials of a social responsibility other than to make as much money for their stockholders as possible. This is a fundamentally subversive doctrine. If businessmen do have a social responsibility other than making maximum profits for stockholders, how are they to know what it is?[1]

Since from this point of view the shareholders bear a firm-specific risk, they are granted a specific claim. After compensating all the demands of the business partners and employees, the shareholders have claim to the residual profit. This can be distributed in the form of dividends, or held back with the result of increasing the value of the shares. In any case, the value for the shareholders should be increased if possible, thereby 'maximizing shareholder value'.

This brings us back to the manager's morning confession. He is the prototype of pure economic thinking, a representative of the financial model. When we speak of this financial model and its meaning, we need to remember that it is purely an economic model based on specific assumptions. Simplified assumptions are often made so that unruly and complex reality can be reduced to precise and clear inter-relationships. The coherence with reality and the significance of such models stands and falls with the assumptions. If the assumptions are wrong or consider only a limited part of reality, then the model should be applied with considerable caution.

In the grand design model, the shareholders are regarded as the only corporation risk bearers, and the capital as the strategically relevant resource. These two assumptions of the model are particularly relevant for our question, namely who are the most important stakeholders for a corporation:

1. *The shareholders as professional risk bearers*: The only group that from a narrow economic point of view bear the corporation risk

are the shareholders. All other stakeholder groups are regulated by complete contracts; meaning also that the benefits and risks of these stakeholders can be formulated and compensated for in some way, independently of whether the activities of the corporation are successful or not.

2. *The capital is the strategically relevant resource*: From this economic perspective, capital is decisive for the strategic success of

a corporation, as it is the base on which every kind of corporation activity is built. The guidelines of corporation activity are therefore based on the expectations of the owners of its capital.

## Basics of stakeholderism

From a stakeholder perspective, in contrast to a purely financial model, there are different risk bearers and different strategically relevant resources. This perspective allows you to grasp a more complex view of reality, and one which is more objective at the same time:

1. *All stakeholders bear possible firm-specific risks*: Not only do the shareholders make firm-specific investments, but also other groups do. There are suppliers who manufacture products that are specific to one buyer. The producer of seats for Porsche is such an example. If there were no demand for Porsches or the corporation were to go bankrupt, then this supplier would suffer as well. Through its firm-specific investment in Porsche, it bears a firm-specific risk. The same can be said for the employees and other stakeholders.
2. *Knowledge, experience, relationships, etc. are also strategically relevant resources*: Capital alone is not decisive for the strategic success of a corporation. According to the industry and the situation, completely different resources may be in the foreground. Empirical investigations have shown that in today's competitive markets, knowledge is strategically more important than obtaining financial capital in order to distinguish oneself from business rivals and in order to survive. Therefore it is not surprising from this point of view that law firms, advertising agencies or consulting companies have very often joined groups of partners together with highly specific knowledge and relationship networks. Their professional qualities, and not their capital investment, are what count strategically. Corporations such as these are primarily dependent on knowledge resources.

If you are following this argument, it is clear that the stakeholder perspective in today's knowledge-based society appears closer to reality than the purely financial model.

## Stakeholder management at stake

As with every approach, stakeholder management has specific risks but also potential benefits:
The risks:

- With the stakeholder approach you are drawing into your deliberations the whole complexity of reality. For the broad spectrum of your differentiated considerations, you need more comprehensive information and new indicators which have neither the long tradition nor the unequivocal acceptance of shareholder value.
- It will be more difficult to satisfy short-term speculators and the analysts of the 'subito-generation'.
- You will have to deal with the fact that a corporation is not just an economic institution but also an important actor in today's interconnected society. Such considerations can be time-consuming and inconvenient.

The opportunities:

- Stakeholder management strives for a comprehensive view of strategic management. It faces the complexities of the everyday reality of your corporation and encourages being in touch with that reality.
- Stakeholder management considers not only the risk but also the possible benefit potential of various stakeholder relationships. Without a systematic stakeholder orientation, you miss strategically relevant value-creation potential for business opportunities which in the final analysis is at the expense of your shareholders.
- Many customers, government agencies and other business partners expect you to encourage good and successful stakeholder relationships. These build trust and acceptance, and opportunities for future collaboration. We have already mentioned that banks, when giving credit to businesses, look to see how they are embedded with their stakeholders. Conscious stakeholder management can affect business benefits.
- You attract the attention of shareholders interested in long-term investments, such as institutional investors.
- On the basis of a systematic analysis of the benefits and risk potentials that lie in stakeholder relationships, you have a tool that can

enable you to stand up successfully to competition, because you are better able to understand how and with whom the corporation's value creation comes about.

## Stakeholder mapping

Our investigations show that so far there are still relatively few corporations which have systematically mapped out their stakeholders. This topic has been of great interest in previous research on stakeholder management, and has resulted in the differentiation of the following categories:

First, the difference between primary and secondary stakeholders is made on the basis of the extent to which individual stakeholders enhance the survival or success of your corporation. Mainly shareholders, customers, suppliers and regulators are named as primary stakeholders. This difference, however, makes a distinction in only an overall manner, and is often too general in practice.

In another area of the literature, it is assumed that stakeholders have specific characteristics such as power, legitimacy and urgency as their main concern. According to our conclusions, in practice corporations are interested primarily in the power and influence that the stakeholder could exert on them. Also they are often interested in what kind of power is coupled with what kind of concern. For example, the customer couples consumer power and economic concerns; the shareholder, his or her role in decision-making and ownership interests. Such relational patterns are shown in Table 2.1. It goes without saying that the complexity of reality does not always allow a clear classification.

Along with power, stakeholders also need legitimacy in order to justify their concerns. Such legitimacy can be based on legal authority or on recognized social norms. In addition, the urgency of the concern plays a role. Stakeholders with all three characteristics rank first in their importance for a corporation. Similarly important are those who have power and legitimacy. In contrast, those stakeholders that have power but lack legitimacy, as for example the Mafia as stakeholder in a pizzeria in Sicily, are very problematic. Also problematic are stakeholders with legitimate concerns but who have little power to accomplish them. A typical example is the native inhabitants of

*Table 2.1*  Characteristics of stakeholders

| 'Stake'/power | Voting power | Economic power | Political power |
| --- | --- | --- | --- |
| Equity stake | • Stockholders<br>• Directors<br>• Minority interests | | • Dissident stockholders |
| Economic stake | • Debt holders<br>• Unions | • Suppliers<br>• Debt holders<br>• Customers<br>• Unions | • Local governments<br>• Foreign governments<br>• Consumer groups<br>• Unions |
| Influence stake | • Government<br>• Outside directors | | • NGOs<br>• Government<br>• Trade associations |

*Source*: Based on Freeman (1984), p. 83.

an ecologically sensitive region in which a corporation aims at tapping natural resources. Such stakeholders – though their claims are legitimate – hardly have a chance to be heard. One therefore calls them 'silent voices'.

In corporations which already maintain long-lasting relationships with individual stakeholders, it is advisable to supplement the diagram in Figure 2.1 with the consideration of 'legacy'. Because of the legacy of the past, a relationship could be either particularly good or bad. This can have strategic implications. Despite a turbulent start, it is known that Geigy (now part of Novartis) had good, long-term relationships with its ecological stakeholders. In critical strategic developmental phases, these good relationships were of great importance.

Our investigations of stakeholder-oriented corporations have shown that these characteristics, which demonstrate the importance of stakeholders quite accurately, are hardly ever considered by corporations. Systematic mapping in this regard is rarely made. However, our carrying out such analyses with corporations gave rise to fruitful discussions, and resulted in some interesting insights and important possibilities for differentiating between various stakeholder types.

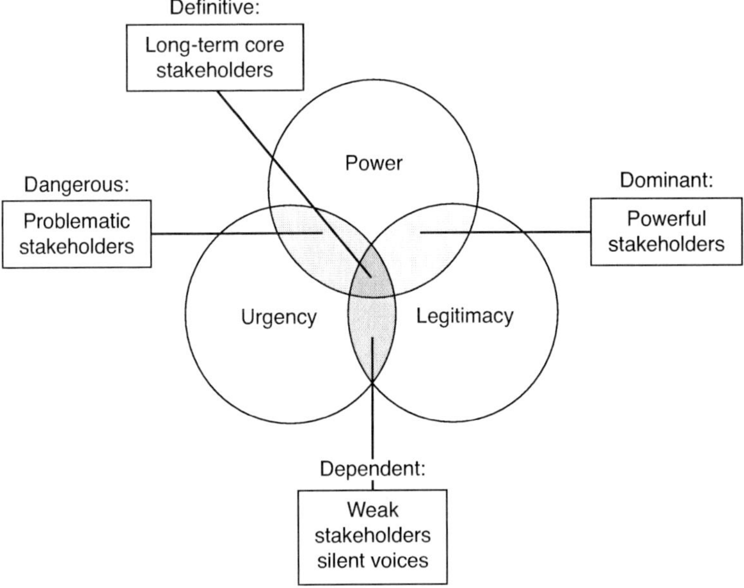


*Figure 2.1*   Stakeholders with two or three key attributes
*Source*: Based on Mitchell, Agle and Wood (1997).

Your task is to make sure that professional stakeholder identification can be carried out for your corporation. Every corporation should have a general or issue specific stakeholder map as an important management tool.

Only occasionally was the implementation of stakeholder mapping confirmed by our interview partners:

'For me, it was an attempt to list my most important stakeholders. Actually I have always done this when dealing with different processes. I want to know who my customers are. I talk about customers and less about stakeholders, but of course they are the same.'

'We have already launched it. In a work group, we started to put together our most important stakeholders. We went through them twice to make sure we had them all and the right ones ... and pretty soon we had the feeling that we had got where we wanted to be. However, we didn't regard these as strategic stakeholders. ... We then said, we want to map who the stakeholder is, how we deal with them, how large this stakeholder group is, whether we are aware of the concerns of this group etc. How are we organized internally, is there a budget for it, are there people that are paying attention to this and how is it dealt with? This is actually the process we are in now.'

Our research also shows that most corporations do not identify and analyse their strategically relevant stakeholders systematically. This is, however, an essential condition for fully tapping the potential benefits that lie in stakeholder relationships, and if a corporation can

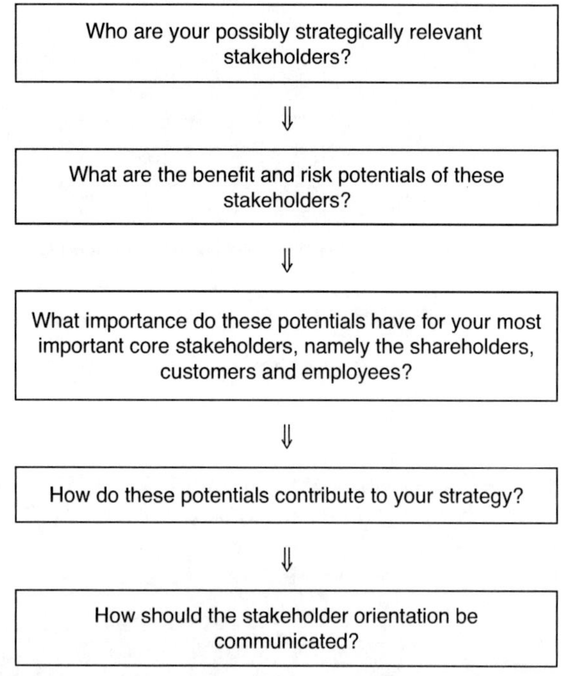


*Figure 2.2*   Systematic analysis of the most important stakeholders

use the potential benefits better than its competitors, then it has a better chance of being more successful than its competitors.

## A ladder to stakeholder potential

For a systematic analysis of the particularly important stakeholders, in your case there are a series of questions:

### Stakeholders – your co-strategists

There are a great many possible stakeholders. The diagram in Figure 2.3 below is provided to help you choose the most relevant ones in a first round.

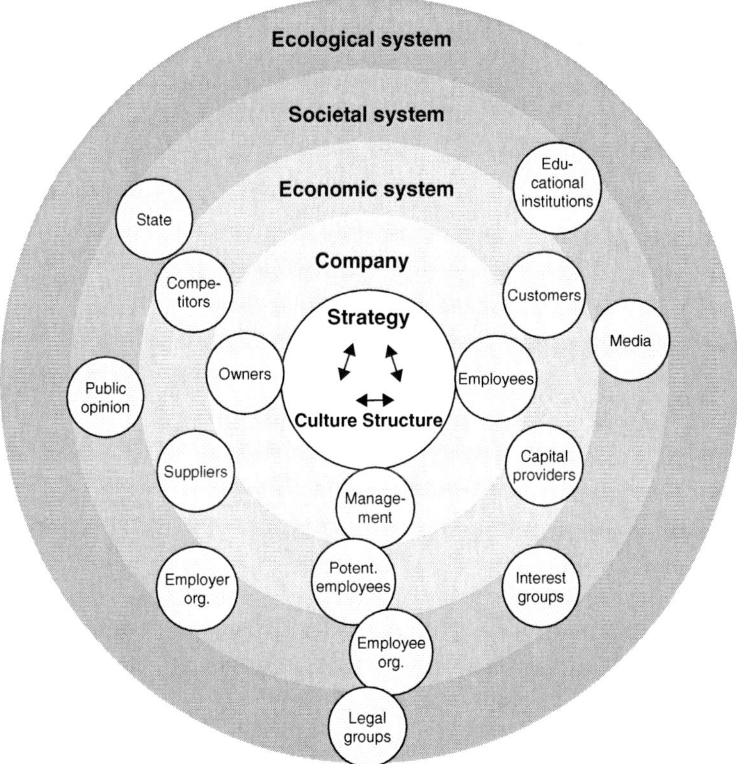


*Figure 2.3*  Possible strategically relevant stakeholders

In our work with corporations, we have found that in clarifying the question of which are the really important stakeholders, discussions have been very productive. In other words, you need to speak with your executive management or departments about which stakeholders are relevant in their eyes. Discuss, for instance, whether all customers are equally relevant, or whether you should form subgroups of various kinds, such as private and business clients.

In a second round, you could additionally submit your findings to either an external or internal specialist for critical review. Often this results in further insights, so that at the end of the round of discussions there is a reassessed joint understanding of who the really relevant stakeholders are, and which one to concentrate on.

### Enhancing benefit or reducing risk potentials

After you have surveyed your stakeholders and their general importance, in a second step you need to focus on analysing which roles they play in the value creation process. In so doing, there are four basic possibilities:

1. *Benefit providers*: These stakeholders render services to the corporation by contributing in some way to the value creation process. Employees contribute by providing specialized knowledge. Suppliers give the corporation a competitive advantage by providing specialized skills or special delivery conditions. Environmental organizations discuss how products can be manufactured and disposed of ecologically, thereby avoiding costs and possibly enabling new uses.

2. *Benefit receivers*: From this perspective, the stakeholders receive additional benefits from the corporation. For example, the customer is offered better service. Pfizer changed its approach to its customers – doctors – by no longer sending sales representatives but instead sending specialists for specific indications to introduce specialized products. Employees may take a continuing education course free of charge during office hours. The local community receives support for an exhibition or project. For various reasons (trust building, improving business relations, etc.), a corporation can be interested in particular concessions. In analysing

the telecom corporations, we noticed that because of the intense competition, all competitors spoke effusively about the services they intended to offer to their customers.

3. *Risk bearers*: At the beginning of this chapter, we have seen that all stakeholders have a firm-specific investment, which means they are risk bearers. As a rule they take on risks consciously. However, there are also stakeholders who involuntarily or unintentionally or even forcibly become risk bearers. An example is Mrs Smith in Chapter 1, who lives near an airport, and because of changes in flight paths has become an unintentional risk bearer.

4. *Risk providers*: Finally, there are stakeholders who create risks for the corporation. Unions can threaten with strikes, NGOs can cause headlines about a corporation's conduct in a developing country, shareholders can bring about resolutions and activate the media or customers can litigate against a corporation. While disposing of the Brent Spar oil platform, Shell experienced the consequences of neglecting a possible risk provider, in this case Greenpeace (see Chapter 7).

Table 2.2 illustrates the results of analysing the role of stakeholders in the value creation process.

This analysis of the benefit and risk potentials can be completed as an internal corporation project or by bringing in an external expert.

*Table 2.2*  Benefit and risk potential of stakeholders (examples)

| Stakeholder | Benefit potential | | Risk potential | |
|---|---|---|---|---|
| | **Provider** | **Receiver** | **Provider** | **Bearer** |
| Stakeholder 1: Customer | Exclusive information on advantages / disadvantages of products and services | High-quality products and services | Negative remarks on products and services $\Rightarrow$ image damage | Defective products |
| Stakeholder 2: Supplier | Exclusive supply and services | Guaranteed sales | Deficient supply | Specific investments for customers |

Giving the analysis a broader base and asking representatives of the respective stakeholder groups how they see the benefits and risks might be of particular interest. These perceptions could then be compared with your own analysis to gain further insights based on the similarities and differences.

Pfizer decided to evaluate the perception of all their strategically relevant stakeholders regarding the benefit and risk potentials. A neutral party started by conducting interviews with Pfizer's stakeholders to evaluate their perceptions of the risk and benefit potentials. In this phase, it was crucial that the interviews were conducted by a neutral mediator. In this role, our research team received all the data that was necessary to understand the overall stakeholder network perspective. Each of the parties was ensured through a statement of confidentiality that the data collected from them would only be shared with another party (stakeholder) if they agreed. This allowed the research team to collect comprehensive data. It also provided the basis for identifying similarities and differences of the perceptions of each stakeholder group. These were then carefully mapped.

For Pfizer, the essential gain is to have acquired transparency and knowledge about a complex environment and the stakeholder network in which it is embedded. Of particular importance for the company is the understanding of which benefit and risk potentials regarding specific issues are present in these stakeholder relationships, and how to evaluate their potentials. In this respect, Pfizer has sharpened its awareness for an increased stakeholder orientation, and was able to acquire the knowledge necessary for handling such a stakeholder orientation in a better way.


## The magic triangle

The shareholders, customers and employees are known, as already mentioned, as the magic triangle of stakeholder management. They are core stakeholders of primary importance, since no corporation can exist without them. In this sense they are constitutive. We have seen in the practical examples that these three stakeholder categories are often anchored in the corporation's vision and mission. For this reason, their opinions are especially relevant for you and will be given a closer look in the analytic steps that follow.

The relevance of the core stakeholders is confirmed by an interview partner:

> 'I always make a model of three elements. In a closed loop, I try to weigh all of them equally, namely the customers, the shareholders and the employees. These are my three most important stakeholders. When I lead or launch a project, I expect my team members always to strive in whatever way possible for harmony within this triangle.'

After internal analyses, in a next step you can have the different benefit and risk potentials mentioned above weighed according to the stakeholder groups in the relevant areas. In our work with corporations, we have found that this leads to particularly interesting insights. The prioritizing of the benefit and risk potentials from the perspective of the different stakeholders of the magic triangle is often controversial. You not only see which stakeholders of the magic triangle are most often judged, for example with high benefit and risk potentials, but from this perspective, you also see the currently most relevant stakeholders for the corporation's value creation process. For an overview Table 2.3 below may be helpful.

*Table 2.3*  Prioritizing the benefit and risk potentials

| Benefit and risk potentials of stakeholders | Weighing by shareholders | Weighing by customers | Weighing by employees | Total |
|---|---|---|---|---|
| Benefit potential 1 (Stakeholder 1) | 5 | 10 | 8 | 23 |
| Benefit potential 2 (Stakeholder 4) | 7 | 6 | 6 | 19 |
| Risk potential 1 (Stakeholder 3) | 2 | 1 | 0 | 3 |
| Risk potential 2 (Stakeholder 3) | 1 | 3 | 0 | 4 |

(Values range from 1 to 10, with 10 as maximum)

Once clearly recognized and evaluated, the individual stakeholders can be investigated in more depth. In this sense, we will come back to the shareholders in Chapter 3, to the customers in Chapter 4 and to the employees in Chapter 5. In addition, we will discuss the importance of industry-specific stakeholders at the end of Chapter 5.

### Impact on strategy

The next step is an explanation of the extent to which these benefit and risk potentials can contribute to the development and implementation of your corporate strategy. Three possibilities are to be considered:

1. From the potential of the stakeholders one gains capital, knowledge, experience and other essential resources, which provide the corporation with the possibility of building up and expanding core competences. Stakeholder relationships can have the effect of enhancing core competence (see Chapter 6).
2. Stakeholders also cultivate relationships among themselves. Your corporation can use this network in the context of its own strategy, in positioning itself to competitive advantage. Stakeholder relationships can therefore have an active and successful positioning effect (see Chapter 7).
3. As already mentioned, corporations are increasingly exposed to public criticism. This means that corporations are continually confronted with new societal expectations. The corporation has to deal with these expectations, in order to obtain and secure a positive position in society. In this way, stakeholder relations have an effect on acceptance (see Chapter 8).

The chart in Table 2.4 illustrates how the benefit and risk potentials of the individual stakeholder relationships contribute to the strategic cornerstones of core competences, positioning and societal acceptance.

As an example, Pfizer Switzerland sees the benefit potential of its strategic stakeholders overwhelmingly in opportunities for successful cooperation and better information. Figure 2.4 shows the ranking of benefit and risk potentials for Pfizer Switzerland.

*Table 2.4*   Contribution to strategic cornerstones

| Benefit and risk potential | Contribution to strategy | | |
| --- | --- | --- | --- |
| | Core competences | Positioning | Societal acceptance |
| Benefit potential 1 (Stakeholder 1) | Knowledge | Cooperation | Goodwill of local authorities |
| Benefit potential 5 (Stakeholder 1) | Trust | Possibility to influence | Stakeholder lobbying for the corporation |
| Risk potential 2 (Stakeholder 3) | Lack of transparency | Little cooperation | Negative effect due to stakeholder 3 |
| Risk potential 6 (Stakeholder 2) | Untrustworthy | Little possibility to influence | High corporation exposure due to some of your stakeholders |

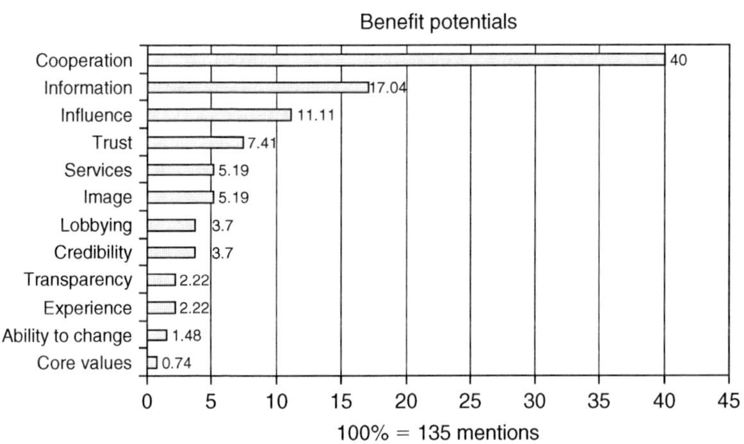


*Figure 2.4*   The benefit potentials as perceived by Pfizer Switzerland

From the chart in Figure 2.5 it appears that Pfizer Switzerland sees a particularly high risk in that, despite its effort to develop interactions, it may not be possible to influence the stakeholders for cooperation.

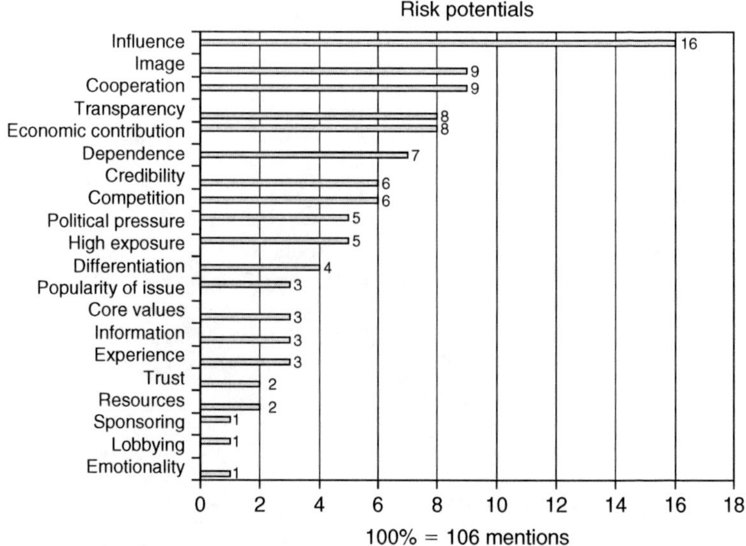


*Figure 2.5*    The risk potentials as perceived by Pfizer Switzerland

## Let's talk about it

When management is comprehensive, meaning the inclusion of the stakeholders, then it is essential to make this transparent to all interested stakeholders. Today a comprehensive sustainability report is important for a constructive stakeholder dialogue, but also as the basis for subsequent strategic considerations within the corporation. In this connection, one often speaks of a triple bottom line. This means that the corporation has not only an economic performance record, but also a social and ecological one. Your corporation should be informed about these three aspects of performance.

In order to fulfil the need for broader reporting, various new indicators in theory and practice have been developed. They will be dealt with in depth further on (see Chapter 10).

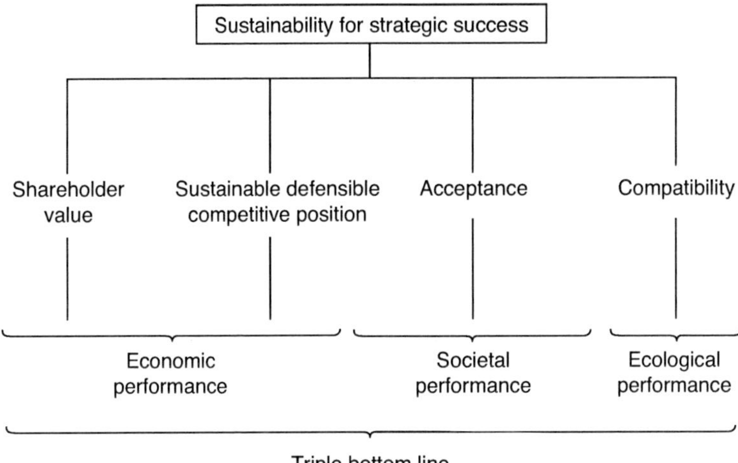


*Figure 2.6* The Triple Bottom Line

The following motto summarizes this chapter:

**Professional stakeholder management (mapping and analysis) leads to important strategic insights for enhancing benefits and reducing risks.**

In order to take advantage of this opportunity, you can ask yourself the following five important questions about your corporation:

1. Who are the most important stakeholders for my corporation?
2. Which are the benefit and risk potentials of these stakeholders?
3. What do these potentials mean for my core stakeholders, namely the shareholders, customers and employees?
4. What contribution do these potentials make to my corporation's strategy?
5. How should the stakeholder orientation be communicated?

| 20 | 21 | 22 | 23 | Goal |
|----|----|----|----|------|
| 19 | 18 | 17 | 16 | 15 |
| 10 | 11 | 12 | 13 | 14 |
| 9 | 8 | 7 | 6 | 5 |
| Start | 1 | 2 | 3 | 4 |

## Shareholder dice game

Relax with a game of dice:

You have just become the CEO of a big corporation. Since the shareholders are mostly unknown to you, you need to demonstrate to them that you are in a position to increase the shareholder value and to overcome everyday stumbling blocks on the way to success.

*Square 3*: As the new CEO, you address your employees for the first time and assure them that for you they are the most important stakeholders in the corporation. Your shareholders react sceptically to your speech. Miss your turn once.

*Square 5*: The annual result of your corporation is the all time best. Move forward three squares.

*Square 7*: You launch a profit-enhancing programme and rationalize away a quarter of your employees. The shares of your corporation jump. Take another turn.

*Square 10*: You have a big sales contract on the hook. Unfortunately you cannot accept it, because now you suddenly have too few people. Move back to Square 2.

*Square 13*: You force a new contract on your suppliers, which obliges them to produce the same quality at less expense. Move forward two squares.

*Square 17*: A customer gives you a hot lead about the technological developments of your customers. For you this is an important reason to innovate. Move forward to Square 23.

*Square 20*: The community president speaks to you, and requests that your factory invest more in means to reduce noise. Move back four squares.

*Square 22*: The shareholders are not satisfied with your financial performance, with the consequence that the board of directors demotes you. Miss your turn twice.

**Goal**: You realize that it is a Sisyphean task to try to satisfy your shareholders. Return to Square 1.

## Note

1   Friedman (1962), p. 133.

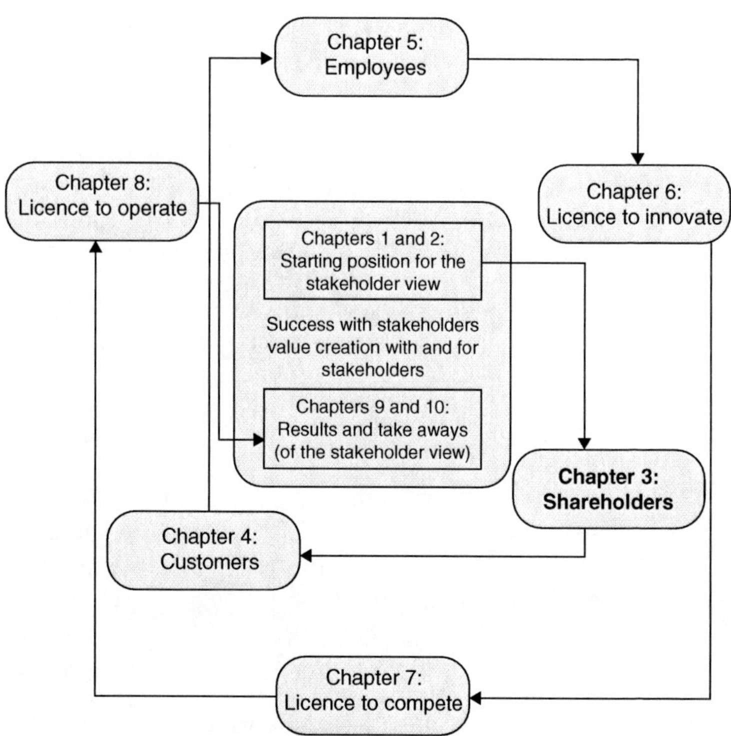

Chapter 5:
Employees
Chapter 8:
Licence to operate
Chapter 6:
Licence to innovate
Chapters 1 and 2:
Starting position for the
stakeholder view
Success with stakeholders
value creation with and for
stakeholders
Chapters 9 and 10:
Results and take aways
(of the stakeholder view)
Chapter 3:
Shareholders
Chapter 4:
Customers
Chapter 7:
Licence to compete

# 3
# Shareholders are also stakeholders

Shareholders are indisputably essential stakeholders of your corporation and should be treated as such by managers.

When semi-annual and annual financial statements come out, corporations are critically examined by investors and their analysts. On such occasions, even if the stated profit is very impressive, the investors still may not necessarily be satisfied. Today it is not only the amount of the profit that is important, but also whether the profit conforms to the continually increasing expectations of investors. Even where high profits are achieved but even higher expectations are not fulfilled, a corporation can still be punished with falling share prices on the stock exchange. 'Any deviation from expectations, positive or negative, can inexplicably mean billions of dollars, more or less, in the market capitalization of large corporations.'[1]

---

**Example: Google (the US Internet search engine)**
For the second quarter of 2005, Google reported doubling its turnover and even quadrupling its profit; nonetheless its price on the stock exchange fell by 5%. The reason was that Google's previous successes had always exceeded the expectations of the analysts. The 2005 second-quarter results were again excellent, but this time the analysts had expected more. The penalty followed immediately.[2]

---

Starbucks, the showcase example of corporate success, did not fare any better:

> **Example: Starbucks (the US coffee roaster and retailer)**
> 'Finally, we have Starbucks (NASDAQ: SBUX), which lost nearly five percent today. The king of caffeine reported that June same-store sales increased by six percent, missing the consensus estimate by a percentage point. UBS cited slowing sales momentum as a reason for its downgrade to 'neutral,' and lowered its same-store sales forecast, and lowered earnings estimate. The brokerage also cited a lower than expected boost from new Frappuccino introductions for the downgrade.'[3]

As we already mentioned in the last chapter, the property that shareholders make available in the form of capital plays a special role in the organizational wealth creation process. The importance of property became increasingly crucial with the high demand for capital caused by industrialization.

## Can I have your watch?

Imagine us meeting each other. I find your watch very attractive. If I were to ask you to give it to me, you would be astonished by my request. Your behaviour would not be considered the least bit impolite, but my request, brazen. The watch is your property.

Property primarily means having the right to dispose of it. Within the bounds of the law, whoever owns property can dispose of it in the manner he sees fit. Property rights enable acquisition, ownership, use and consumption of things. Non-owners are excluded from having such rights. Today this understanding of property also includes knowledge. One speaks of intellectual property.

The capitalist system is based on this understanding of property. The importance of property is also emphasized by Milton Friedman in his book *Capitalism and Freedom*:

> A still more basic economic area in which the answer is both difficult and important is the definition of property rights. The notion of property, as it has developed over centuries and as it is embodied

in our legal codes, has become so much a part of us that we tend to take it for granted, and fail to recognize the extent to which just what constitutes property and what rights the ownership of property confers are complex social creations rather than self-evident propositions.[4]

For corporations, from a stakeholder point of view primarily two problems regarding property are in the forefront:

1. The relationship of owner and manager
2. The creation of value for the owner.

## How to regulate the conflict between shareholder and management – a rocky relation

Industrialization and the rationalization that accompanied it released an enormous process of growth, which for many corporations led to an equivalent increase in size. There are corporations such as Shell whose revenue (almost $319 billion in 2006) is comparable to the GDP of a small country, such as Austria (GDP $322 billion in 2006). The larger a corporation is, the less likely it is that the owner and the manager are the same person, such as was the case formerly with founder corporations. The original constellation can be found most frequently in family corporations. With a publicly owned corporation, however, there is a separation of ownership and control. This separation is problematic because the profitability demands of the shareholders and the interests of management often contradict each other. External shareholders are often primarily interested in a high rate of return and maintaining their investment. Managers are more interested in the possibility of developing professionally, and maybe also in the power and prestige of their position plus the amount of their bonuses. In the context of corporate governance, coming to terms with these conflicting aims is often a main concern. Within the chain of command, one needs to clarify how the influence of shareholders is to be regulated, how the management body is to be constituted and what legal regulations are necessary. On an international level, examples of this are the legally determined US Sarbanes–Oxley Act (2002) and the 2002 OECD Guidelines (Organisation for Economic Co-operation and Development) as a code of conduct for 'Best Practices of Good Corporate Governance.'

In this chapter, with this background in mind, we want to discuss the importance of shareholder engagement. In doing so from a stakeholder perspective, the shareholder in the context of basic legal principles[5] should be increasingly bound into strategic discussions and understood as a genuine stakeholder.

**The pay back**

An approach concerned with creating and measuring value creation is value-based management. The basic of value-based management is the shareholder value, meaning the dividends and the share price. From this perspective, projects and also whole strategies are judged on the basis of the economic benefit they generate for the providers of capital. If there is a choice among several strategic alternatives, the choice is made for the one promising the greatest increase in shareholder value. As already mentioned in Chapter 1, shareholder value-based management is a highly accepted practice in the USA, and in recent years has also gained increased importance in Europe.

As its premise, this approach sees all the owners (shareholders) as having the same uniform interest regarding increased value. However, in reality this is often not the case. The interests of individual shareholder categories are known to be as divergent as those of owner and management. Shareholders may have long-term and entrepreneurial interests, like the shareholders of a family corporation; or they may follow short-term speculative interests, like day-traders. The latter try to recognize daily variations and to exploit them, which is why they make only short-term investments. In between lie many degrees of variation. Managers might be interested in a one-sided development of the share value, if their remunerations are linked with it. In addition to short-term success, institutional investors also often have the protection of their investment in mind; and business partners may invest in corporations in order to maintain their primary suppliers or customers. This is confirmed by Stout:[6]

> Different shareholders have different time frames, different tax concerns, different attitudes toward firm-level risk due to different levels of diversification, different interests in other investments that might be affected by corporate activities, and different views about the extent to which they are willing to sacrifice corporate

profits to promote broader social interests, like a clean environment or good wages for workers. These and other schisms ensure that there is no single, uniform measure of shareholder 'wealth' to be 'maximized'.

In the same article, Stout concludes from a legal standpoint that 'shareholder wealth maximization is not a modern legal principle'. Rather, she confirms that in the USA a 'large majority of state codes contain so-called other-constituency provisions that explicitly authorize corporate boards to consider the interests of not just shareholders, but also employees, customers, creditors, and the community, in making business decisions'.[7]

As a result, the shareholders of a corporation are by no means a homogeneous group with the same values and goals, thus hindering the creation of value for all of the shareholders.

A special case is when a firm is a subsidiary of a parent corporation, possibly with international business interests. In this situation, the influence of one shareholder alone is very direct. As a rule, it is not limited to the competences and responsibilities of the corporation organs. Usually it exists alongside a wide variety of specialized and managerial influences of the parent corporation. For these managers of the subsidiary entirely different ownership problems from the ones mentioned above arise.

On the one hand, they have a stable ownership situation and thereby predictable ownership influences factors without the daily fluctuations in the stock market price; at least as long as the subsidiary is an associate of the parent corporation and has not been sold off. Often these managers can profit in financial considerations from the specialized knowledge of the parent corporation or from its stronger position in the capital market. They are spared expensive investor-relationship activities. On the other hand, they have to deal with the positive and negative influences of the parent corporation, as was the case for Orange Switzerland.

---

**Example: Orange (Swiss Telecom Corporation):**
At Orange, a subsidiary of France Télécom, there was significant pressure in 2003 to deliver cash on short notice, because the parent corporation was badly in debt.

> 'The pressure was big. We had the feeling we were being
> squeezed like a lemon financially. The numbers we were
> delivering were good, and so were the results. But still we
> had to push and pressure our people, and tell them they
> had to produce more and deliver more, even though we
> were actually working profitably and doing good business
> in our own terms.'

Particularly attractive for the corporation and its management are those shareholders that associate themselves with a corporation in the long term, and that are not out for short-term speculative profits. When you have shareholders with a long-term interest in your corporation, then as manager you are more likely to be able to pursue a sustainable and successful strategy.

Studies by Credit Suisse and MorganStanley show how important and profitable good shareholder relations can be. Both looked at the performance of family corporations, for example those in which the founding corporation still exerts a large influence. Credit Suisse came to the conclusion that since 1996 in Europe these corporations regularly supersede the competition. MorganStanley determined that those corporations which figure in the S&P 500 in the years 2000–2005 superseded its index. For Credit Suisse, there were three main reasons for the better–than-average performance: 'A management focus oriented to the longer term, better alignment between management and shareholder interests, and a stronger focus on core business'.[8]

Also Socially Responsible Investing offers some interesting solutions.

## Investing in the future

In Socially Responsible Investing (SRI) shareholders, investors and analysts judge capital investments specifically on the basis of financial criteria, but also to a significant extent on societal and ecological criteria. In addition, they have a long-term perspective. In order that sustainable investors can inform themselves, corporations have to report not only their financial but also their social and ecological activities. In Europe, in 2005 €1033 billion were invested in sustainable assets. By comparison, in 2003 it was only €336 billion. This corresponds to a growth of over 200 per cent.[9] Corporations with a good reputation regarding social and ecological criteria are in an advantageous position to attract capital.

Every year in the USA, *Business Ethics Magazine* selects the '100 Best Corporate Citizens'. Corporations are ranked according to criteria such as environment, human rights, employee relations and governance. The ranking for 2007 is as follows:

1. Green Mountain Coffee Roaster
2. Advanced Micro Devices
3. Nike
4. Motorola
5. Intel Corporation[10]

In talking with corporations, one is surprised at times by how narrowly the demands and expectations of the investors are still seen. The short-term striving of managers for shareholder value is an expression of it. Long-term perspectives are looked upon with great reservations. Blowfield and Googins confirm that CEOs are occasionally willing to acknowledge that the pressure of short-term performance sets limits to the corporation's long-term performance, which serves both the shareholder and societal interests.[11]

A very useful study of the factors which capital investors look at when buying shares shows that investors look at more than merely financial variables when making investment decisions, even if they do not explicitly prescribe to Socially Responsible Investing.[12] The shareholder would appear to be a differentiated, thoughtful stakeholder. The authors of the above-mentioned studies asked experts of investment corporations for the information they use in making their investment decisions. It is absolutely clear that the decision makers always considered non-financial criteria as well. This naturally affects the share price and the cost of capital of a corporation. The study also makes clear that where non-financial criteria are considered, the profits from the investments are higher and the risks lower than in cases where such information is not considered.

The authors found that of the people they questioned, 35 per cent of their investment decisions were based on non-financial information, thus documenting its importance. What non-financial information is considered? According to the study, the accent lies clearly on strategic management behaviour:

1. Implementation of corporate strategy
2. Management credibility
3. Quality of corporate strategy
4. Innovative ability

Since investors are considering societal and ecological criteria more often in making decisions, it has become increasingly worthwhile for corporations to take sustainable thinking into consideration.

An investigation by Deloitte and Euronext[13] shows that social and environmental performance are becoming more important for investors. A majority of the questioned fund managers and financial analysts are of the opinion that interest in SRI investments has increased and that this development will also affect the voting behaviour of investors.

Most corporation reporting gives little evidence of the above-mentioned criteria for the decision making of investors, and even less about the ways society and ecology performance affect strategic development. Such information, however, will be highly relevant for investors if they are to be won over to an increasingly sustainable way of thinking. There are exceptions, such as among insurance corporations, as demonstrated by Swiss Re.

---

**Example: Swiss Re**
Concerning sustainability, Swiss Re has a leading position. The reason is not astonishing, since Swiss Re is embedded in the polarity between sustainable, long-term business interests and short-term profit for investors. In the reinsurance business, transactions are often completed whose consequences

sometimes cannot be fully known for another 20 or more years. Because of such long-term perspectives, Swiss Re is particularly dependent on a healthy, stable financial basis. Shareholders are especially relevant stakeholders, since capital is an extremely important strategic resource for a business-like reinsurer. Therefore it would be of importance for Swiss Re if their shareholders were consciously to acquire a sustainable orientation. In addition to the intention of making long-term investments, this orientation would need to include an expressed appreciation of the ecological and societal risks. This stands in contrast to those investors who want to see a profit at the end of each quarter, and who have shown little interest in the long-term business of Swiss Re. The reaction of those investors was revealed a year after Swiss Re was faced with a number of extreme catastrophes, such as hurricane Katrina (28 August 2005). Although Swiss Re was able to show a profit at the end of the year, it was not as high as had been forecast. The consequence was a fall in share prices. As a result, it was in Swiss Re's interest to demonstrate the long-term nature of the business, and to show the sustainable strategic income possibilities in spite of short-term fluctuations.

Despite the high growth rates of SRI in the past years in Europe, as mentioned above, on the whole the supply of sustainable, that is to say socially responsible, investing is still meagre at present. In the USA, for example, 11 per cent of all professional investments are in keeping with SRI.

In mid 2005 there were 375 green, social and ethical funds, which represented a 6 per cent growth in relation to the previous year. In 1980 there were only four such funds; the number has grown continuously since then.

Socially Responsible Investing is also an active investment strategy and is therefore connected with increased shareholder engagement with the corporation. This leads to a greater convergence of the interests of such broadly engaged shareholders with the interests of other stakeholders.

## Shareholder engagement

Shareholders have two well-known strategies when they are dissatisfied with the corporation that they have invested in. They can withdraw from their engagement (Exit Strategy) or they can try through dialogue to exert influence (Voice Strategy or Shareholder Engagement).

Shareholder engagement includes three activities according to current understanding:

1. Shareholders actively use their voting rights at annual meetings.
2. Shareholders place their own proposals on the agenda.
3. There are informal meetings among large investors (e.g. pension funds) and corporations on the subject of sustainability (economic themes, corporate governance themes, and environmental and social themes).

Among the reasons for an increasing interest in widespread shareholder engagement are the corporate scandals of the recent past. In the USA, Enron and WorldCom are the best known examples; in Europe, Parmalat. Similar scandals have also occurred in various other countries. What these scandals have in common is that the top managers were all able to assert their personal interests, such as power and greed, in a shocking manner without being checked by either shareholders or supervisory bodies, such as boards of directors. As Bogle states with regard to the situation in the USA, the representatives of ownership failed as did other stakeholders in their surveillance function:

> Despite being the elected representatives of the owners, boards of directors looked on the proceedings with benign neglect, apparently unmindful of the impending storm. Lightning first struck Enron. When the firm collapsed in November 2001, the *New York Times* described it as a 'catastrophic corporate implosion … that encompassed the company's auditors, lawyers, and directors … regulators, financial analysts, credit rating agencies, the media, and Congress … a massive failure in the governance system.' Other dominoes soon fell, including WorldCom, Adelphia, Global Crossing, and Tyco. In the years that followed, still more disreputable companies were to surface.[14]

Market mechanisms also failed: the invisible hand of the market is supposed to transform the personal interests of top managers into the general interest of society. In many countries, there are overall hardly more than 1000 executives who sit in the governing bodies of the important corporations. As a result, these executives can support each other's personal interests. In fact, in this exclusive circle, the various personal interests are joined to form a 'common interest' though this is usually only for those directly concerned. Therefore, it is not the job market that sets the cost (or compensation) of the managers but rather a limited clan, and the choice of managers is also not according to the supply of those available, but rather according to a select circle of handpicked people.

**Example: Nestlé (Swiss food corporation)**
At the Annual Meeting of Nestlé in 2005, the Chief Executive Officer also wanted to become the President of the Board of Directors as the current one was retiring. The Investment Foundation Ethos opposed this request, and was supported by the ISS (Institutional Shareholder Services) in the USA, which represents over 1000 institutional investors. When the corporate CEO heard of the resistance to his election, he threatened that he and the whole Nestlé Board of Directors would resign if he were not elected President. At the time of his candidacy as President of the Board, the CEO was also Vice President of the Board of Credit Suisse.[15]

## Pension funds as global investors

A further reason for increased shareholder engagement is the so-called 'financial intermediaries', such as pension funds and investment funds of all kinds. Robert Monk, the most well-known shareholder activist in the world, calls these institutions the new global investors. How come? In the USA, the largest industrial nation, they administer over half of all assets. Bogle reports that 'institutional investors of all types – public and private retirement funds, mutual funds, endowment funds, and bank trust departments – now own 66 percent of all US equities'.[16] However, for an example from among other countries, in Switzerland about 10–15 per cent of the SMI stock of shares is held by pension funds; it is calculated it will be about 20–25 per cent in 20 years' time. This means that in Switzerland too pension funds will soon be very important investors.

Pension funds hold the money of policy holders in trust. They have a marked interest in long-term business. They are unlikely to sell important shares even when they are not doing so well. It is difficult for them to have an exit strategy. However, if they are inactive in this way, it can have fatal consequences for the policy holders. Here is a possible imaginary scenario:

If, for example, a research-based pharmaceutical corporation is under pressure because of short-term shareholder interests, a consequence might be that the corporation is less inclined to invest in research and development. This would mean that in the long run the corporation would not be able to launch as many new products and would thus become less profitable. In the end, this would have a negative effect on retirement payments to those policy holders of the insurance corporation who had shares in this corporation. For this reason, retirement funds need to be in proactive contact with such corporations. Their chances of being able to exert influence are clearly given.

In this regard, there is indisputably still a lot to be clarified, primarily because managers of investment and pension funds behave passively on the whole in connection with the corporations whose property they manage, and apparently siphon off a large part of the acquired income for themselves.[17] 'Public, private, and individual retirement savings are the backbone of our financial system, but our intermediaries consume far too large a portion of whatever returns our financial markets are generous enough to provide, with far too small a portion going to the last-line investors who put up all of the capital and assume all of the risks.'[18]

A positive example of what we mean is provided by the active investment strategy of the Carbon Disclosure Project.

---

**Example: Carbon Disclosure Project (asset managers of international pension funds)**
In this project, different internationally and globally active asset managers of pension funds joined together and pooled the assets of several billion US dollars. From this position of strength, they got in contact with corporations producing

high $CO_2$ emissions. They asked these corporations to present a strategy for how they planned to reduce the emissions. In this way, cooperation took place between the asset managers and these corporations regarding a specific and highly relevant topic.[19]

**Example: Principles for Responsible Investment (PRI)**
The same can be said for an initiative on the New York and Paris stock exchanges in the spring of 2006, underwritten by 'Principles for Responsible Investment' (PRI). It concerns the pooling of US$4000 billion joint capital by long-term oriented fund managers and institutional investors. They ask corporations to give greater consideration to long-term aspects. PRI expects that banks and brokers provide holistic financial analyses. The investors are of the opinion that in the future there is a need for such topics as corporate governance, the environment and society to have more influence on portfolios. Investors fulfilling their fiduciary duties therefore have to give sufficient consideration to these topics.

### Trend to collaboration

Financial intermediaries should and could address corporation problems more frequently and more actively, and many corporations could pay greater attention to their investor relations, e.g. by organising investor days and allowing extended dialogues. The fact that this has been happening more frequently in recent years makes it possible to speak of a new development in the direction of collaborative engagement. This means the cooperation of investors, pension funds, corporations and other interested persons in a broad application of developmental strategy. In this context, Bogle suggests:

Owners and managers must unite in the task of returning the focus of corporate strategy and corporate information to long-term financial goals, cash flows, intrinsic values, and progress in the development of strategic direction. Quarterly earnings guidance, pernicious yet still omnipresent, should be eliminated, replaced by quarterly reports that cover not only the operations and financial results for the firm but a discussion of significant changes to the long-term business plan; unexpected changes in costs, business volumes, and market share; status of competitive position; and so on.

While all of this information must be publicly disclosed, it is professional analysts and money managers who will most carefully analyse it. Thus, open video meetings of executives with these experts (with publicly available transcripts) should become common. Long-term shareholders who engage in candid communication with management and are cooperative rather than confrontational, describing what they expect from their investment – including what dividends they expect – will play a major role in the restoration of owners' capitalism.[20]

The fact that occasionally negative influence (or even demonstration of power) is exerted by financial intermediaries on the strategy of corporations does not change the manifold advantages of collaborative shareholder engagement. A member of Pfizer's management answered an ensuing question in the following dialogue:

'Q: Naturally, what interests me most from the point of view of the finance group is that one is always discussing the competition between financial performance and social performance, and now that you are planning an increased stakeholder orientation in your corporation, it will have an impact on the finances. How do you see this from the point of view of Pfizer Switzerland?'

'A: Yes, naturally shareholders have that [concern], which is always a big topic. Ultimately it is a business operation, which needs to make profit and is obliged to by the stock market. I wouldn't say that there is much of a conflict in the end. I am convinced that the cost of medicine can be reduced. That would help us and the society, and it would help the whole economy and the whole of health care. I would say that it is always the same interests in the end. The equation is balanced.'

New opportunities could be opening up for you in this area in the future.

On the basis of what we have stated, the following motto can be drawn:

**Shareholders are also stakeholders with differentiated interests, and not only passive anonymous providers of capital.**

From this perspective, you can clarify the following questions for your corporation:

1. Which are the most important shareholder groups of my corporation and what are their interests, commitments and potentials?
2. How do my essential shareholders judge the benefit and risk potential of my other strategically relevant stakeholders?
3. How sustainable or how long-term is the nature of my business? Do I have similarly minded shareholders?
4. How attractive is my business for the category of investors which I am especially seeking?
5. What would communication with the desired investors look like in my concrete case?

## Notes

1 Bogle (2005), p. iii.
2 CNN (2005).
3 Schaeffer (2006).
4 Friedman (1962), p. 26.
5 Cf., for example, OPSI (2002), www.opsi.gov.uk/si/si2002/20021986.htm
6 Stout (2007): p. 10.
7 Stout (2007), pp. 5 and 10.
8 Kalbreier *et al.* (2007), p. 49; McVey *et al.* (2005).
9 Eurosif (2006).
10 Business-Ethics (2007).
11 Blowfield and Googins (2006).
12 Low and Siesfeld (1998).
13 Deloitte and Euronext (2003).
14 Bogle (2005), p. 34.
15 Nestlé (2005); Tages-Anzeiger (2005).

16  Bogle (2005) pp. 5 and 74.
17  Bogle (2005).
18  Bogle (2005), p. xi.
19  Ethos (2006).
20  Bogle (2005), pp. 54–5.

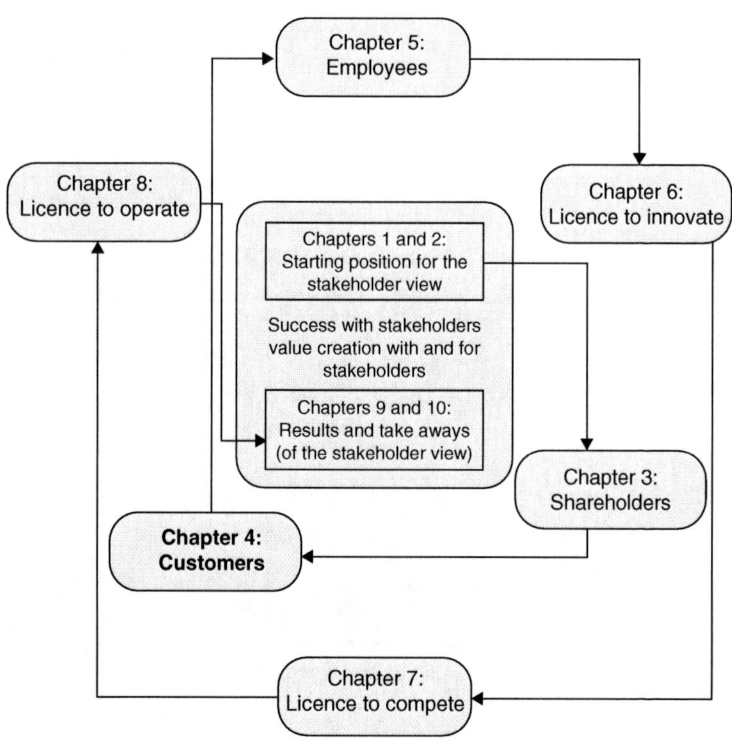

Chapter 5:
Employees
Chapter 8:
Licence to operate
Chapter 6:
Licence to innovate
Chapters 1 and 2:
Starting position for the
stakeholder view
Success with stakeholders
value creation with and for
stakeholders
Chapters 9 and 10:
Results and take aways
(of the stakeholder view)
Chapter 3:
Shareholders
Chapter 4:
Customers
Chapter 7:
Licence to compete

# 4
# Getting to know your customers

We all know the saying: 'the customer is king'. For this reason, meeting the customers' needs is often mentioned as the *raison d'être* of a corporation. Here are some quotes from our case study interviews:

> 'The customers are at the centre of what we do, and regardless of the situation we approach them with a positive attitude and with dedication.'

> 'The first stakeholder for me, and for many of our activities, is the customer. We don't do business if the customer is unsatisfied.'

The paramount importance of the customers is also emphasized by most corporations in their basic documented statements, such as vision or business principles.

In our investigations, two-thirds of the corporations we studied mentioned the customers as the most important stakeholder. For the other third, the customer is a close second. Table 4.1 below clearly shows this.

Repeatedly, interview partners mentioned that in reality the customer orientation is less than it should be. One interview partner put it bluntly:

> 'I think that there is a large discrepancy between claim and reality. In the first place, I don't believe that when you look at what we have done in the past six or seven years, one could say the customers have had a central position in our orientation and in

what we have done. I would argue against the claim that the customers are really the central stakeholder or make up the central stakeholders. It is true that we claim they are, but we don't take this as seriously as we say we do.'

Evidence for how important the effect of a customer orientation would be in practice is provided by a study of the website, Forum for People Performance Management & Measurement (www.performanceforum.org). It shows that there is a direct relationship between employee satisfaction and customer satisfaction, and that there is also a relationship between the commitment of management to their employees and the satisfaction of the customers.

Employee satisfaction has a positive influence on customer satisfaction, whereas the commitment of management to their employees has an indirect influence on customer satisfaction affected by two mechanisms: (1) commitment to employees has a direct positive influence on the level of the market orientation of a corporation ... and (2) by means of its direct influence on the market orientation, employee commitment has an indirect effect on customer behaviour, which again directly influences customer satisfaction.[1]

Applying a customer orientation is not always easy. In the telecommunications industry one can especially see that dealing with customers is still primarily based on a technological rather than a service orientation.

'There is always the conflict between giving the customers what they want and what we can do. However, it is important to take the customers seriously as stakeholders. Also, one needs to ask them what they really want. It doesn't make sense for us to try to change them. There is the slight tendency of saying we have this nice device here, so please be good enough to use it. This won't work or only with a certain segment of customers, namely the techno-freaks and the younger generation. There is the danger with mobile phones that the older generation simply won't use them, because they are too complicated for them.'

An example of underestimating customer know-how is illustrated by the SMS success story: SMS (Short Message Service) is a hit with

*Table 4.1* The most important stakeholders

| Corporation | Corporation 1 | Corporation 2 | Corporation 3 | Corporation 4 | Corporation 5 | Corporation 6 | ø |
|---|---|---|---|---|---|---|---|
| **Frequency customers** | 26.8% | 41.3% | 28.6% | 15.3% | 21.5% | 15.2% | 24.8% |
| **Frequency employees** | 16.9% | 27.2% | 18.4% | 18.2% | 15.2% | 15.4% | 18.6% |
| **Frequency shareholders** | 16.2% | 4.4% | 2.1% | 10.9% | 6.4% | 13.9% | 9.0% |

young consumers. Every generation wants technology that it can adopt to its own needs. The technological generation took to SMS. Paradoxically, the relative complexity of the technology was what appealed to many young people. The entry threshold was high and so parents, teachers and other grown-up authority figures were unable or unwilling to use the service. Young people wanted their own communication technology despite the effort it required.[2]

From a stakeholder perspective, not only are the immediate wishes of the customers relevant but also, from a comprehensive point of view, their opinions as users and consumers. Understood this way, it is obviously important for a corporation to acquaint itself with the knowledge and experience of its customers, and to integrate this in the development of its products and services. One of our interview partners made this statement:

> 'The physician is a determining factor in the pharmaceutical industry for Pfizer Switzerland, because he decides on the appropriate cure for his patients, and so we have to remain in contact with him.'

The annual study by Booz Allen Hamilton[3] shows that customers can make important contributions to the innovative ability of a corporation. In their study, the authors show that financial means alone are no guarantee for the development of successful products and services. It is more important to know what the customers really want. In this regard, those corporations do particularly well that deal actively with their customers and develop new products according to their needs. As an example the authors cite DeWalt, a subsidiary of Black & Decker. For house construction, DeWalt developed a mitre saw that was used on construction sites and was one of the most sold saws. When DeWalt visited a building site in order to see how the saw worked in the real world, they saw that the construction workers could not saw large wooden beams in one step. Together with the customers DeWalt then developed a larger mitre saw which was able to satisfy the customers' needs. Not only was the new saw better; DeWalt could also sell it for a much higher price than the old saws. The customers were so enthusiastic about the new tool that the price was irrelevant and the new mitre saw broke all sales records.[4]

That customers are even more important for the innovative ability of a corporation than its own research department is also illustrated

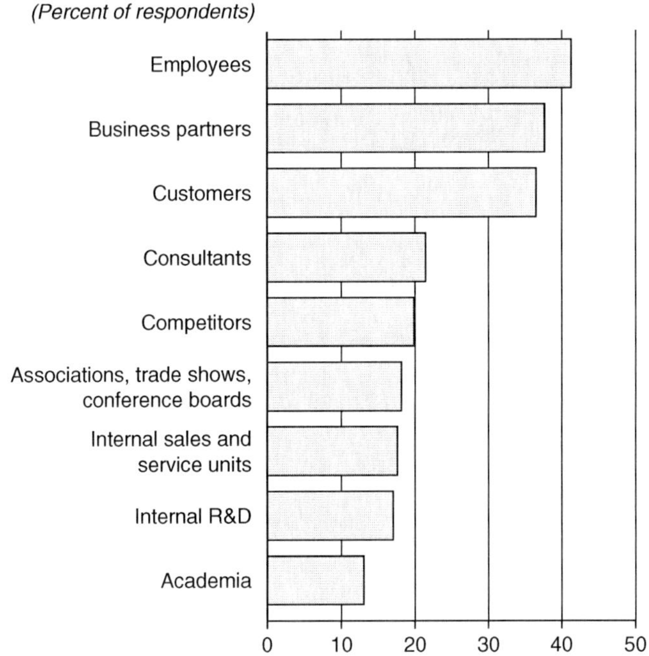



Note: Respondents could select up to three choices

*Figure 4.1*   External stakeholders and special customers are important sources of innovation
*Source*: IBM (2006), p. 24. Reprinted courtesy of International Business Machines Corporation, copyright 2006 © International Business Machines Corporation.

by IBM's *Global CEO Study 2006*. The study is based on questioning over 700 CEOs around the world. The advantages of collaboration with customers are obvious to the CEOs: lower costs, higher profits, greater market availability – to name only a few.[5]

When the experience or knowledge of the customers is not taken into account correctly, then customer relationships (particularly in the USA!) may bear a considerable risk potential, as the following anecdote demonstrates: Michelle Knepper from Vancouver, Washington, chose a specialist from the telephone book for fat suction treatment. She chose a dermatologist who was not a plastic surgeon. When complications set in, she complained that she would never

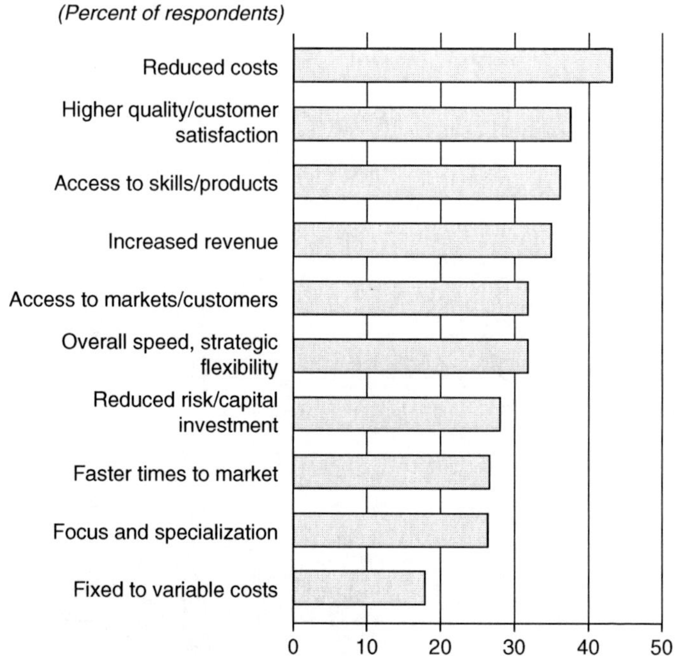


*Figure 4.2* Collaboration with customers provides numerous and varied advantages

*Source*: IBM (2006), p. 27. Reprinted courtesy of International Business Machines Corporation, copyright 2006 © International Business Machines Corporation.

have chosen the specialist had she known that he was not certified for the procedure. (She apparently relied on the telephone book listing rather than asking the specialist.) She sued ... the telephone corporation! And lo and behold, she was awarded USD 1.2 million plus USD 375,000 for her husband's 'loss of marital privileges.'[6]

## No two alike

As we previously saw regarding shareholders, there are also no uniform categories of customers. In practice at present, differentiated categories of customers are of great importance. In many corporations, all customer data are stored in professional databases. This data is then processed so as to be available to the whole corporation at any level, in suitable form and segments. Depending on how a problem is approached, different customer-stakeholder categories can be arranged and handled in a customized manner.

In order to consider customers as a real strategic resource, many corporations have established Customer Relationship Management (CRM). CRM is IT-supported marketing management; the goal is to bind the customer in the long term, to form a deeper interaction and to make respectively higher profits. CRM identifies essential customers and, due to a more professional assessment, gives indications of how their needs can be better satisfied. On this basis, establishing long-term customer relations with existing customers is an integral part of marketing, and today, along with the acquisition of new customers, some corporations are investing a more or less large amount of the marketing budget in customer-relations management. This makes economic sense, since it is usually more profitable to pay attention to existing customers than to acquire new ones.

For the necessary databases, in addition to administrative information, one needs to save the customers' complete customer histories, the type and frequency of transaction and other marketing-specific transactions:

- Matching corporation and customer strategy.
- Clarifying the relevant business processes between customers and corporation.
- Support for CRM from management and the employees.
- Ability to integrate CRM-software in the existing IT system.
- Integration of important customers in CRM.

Often in corporations, the focus of CRM appears to be too narrowly on the processes and technologies. One needs to keep in mind that only a lived customer orientation permits the effective use of CRM. Also one must not overlook the fact that customer behaviour can change, as for example if the customer notices that the corporation is using information excessively. This clearly demonstrates that customers want to be seen as partners and not merely information bearers. This leads us to the next essential question.

## Treating them right

If you work in a large corporation, then you are undoubtedly familiar with the annual, or at least every second year, evaluation of customer satisfaction. With more or less sophisticated techniques, the degrees of satisfaction with the products and services which your corporation offers are collected from the various customer groups. Often one asks if they have any further requests. In some corporations, customer complaints are evaluated systematically, providing in particular information on how the existing product lines or services could be improved to the customers' advantage. Naturally these systems are less able to provide pointers regarding new developments. A number of corporations organize round-tables with top customers or offer conferences for important customers in an effort to introduce them to the newest products and services.

In our case studies, we heard from some of our interview partners that though such customer contact is elegantly celebrated, the contact is rarely systematically evaluated. A systematic evaluation should consider the questions below.

## Customer impact

The most obvious answer to this question is that customers generate revenue by buying the products and services of the corporation; however, looking at things this way is insufficient. In most corporations, far too little attention is paid to seeing the customers as more than a generator of revenue, and to seeing them consciously and systematically not only as benefit receivers but also as benefit providers. This is confirmed by quotations from our interviewees:

> 'We were very successful at a time when other branches of the business were having problems, and it was difficult for anyone to see how the future was going to develop. We brought in our best people and really tried to combine our knowledge with that of our customers. We brought up some interesting things, to which our customers were able to bring in their knowledge. There are really many advantages, when we can join our expertise to theirs. We generated some good ideas. It is a good knowledge network.'

> 'We have customer round tables. When we are developing products, we test them at various stages with our customers; partly also with pilot customers who support us in these processes. There are various activities for broadening customer knowledge.'

'I think that the knowledge providers might be primarily the doctors, the hospitals. I'm also thinking about scientists, key opinion leaders, and in a way maybe the government.'

Regarding the stakeholder-oriented view of customers, and according to the general procedural concept presented in Chapter 2, a corporation is able to elevate the benefit and risk potentials systematically. In a next step, these potentials can be examined further. For example, Swiss Re organizes specialized trade fairs with groups of customers, in which they work out the benefit and risk potentials on the basis of current topics.

This approach has two positive effects:

1. The corporation learns how to integrate better the benefit potentials and/or minimize the risks in its value-creation processes;
2. The corporation can sensitize its customers to the opportunities and threats which exist from its point of view.

Even in close customer contact, our evaluation showed that corporations often concentrate primarily on an exchange of information and less on a common learning process.

## Learning lessons

There are many possibilities for learning with customers:

- Learning by sharing experience: The most frequent kind of learning process with customers is sharing experience with one another.

'Well, of course, the customer needs are central. What products or consultation does he or she want from us? This means that we have to develop the ability to be able to hear what the customer wants and to adapt what we can provide. This seems to me to be of central importance. Then it is important to put ourselves in the position of being able to offer, let's say, at least two or more products to choose from. And finally, the concrete recommendation or finalization by our consultant is important, in order to support the customer in making the right decision. We don't do this as much as we should. We have potential to improve here.'

Certainly this kind of classic customer survey can be a basis for clarifying which products and services and which customer groups to concentrate on. However, it is also essential that those employees who are in constant contact with customers are obliged to engage internally in the systematic sharing and evaluating of their experiences. They should be appropriately compensated if any improvements result from their efforts.

- *Learning by testing*: Microsoft followed the variant of looking for test people for the beta-version of a new software. These customers could use the software free until the complete version was adopted, but they were obligated to give Microsoft feedback on any shortcomings.
- *Collaborative learning*, also called dual creation: In such a case, the knowledge generated with an individual customer on a specific product or specific service may then be transferred to another customer:

> Take the customers of Cisco Systems, the leading manufacturer of equipment for computer networks. After the corporation had recognized the competence of its customers, Cisco set up Cisco Connections Online, which is an outcome of interactive, networked services with quick access to Cisco's information, resources and systems. The network enables Cisco's customers to be in dialogue with each other, in order to help each other solve technical problems and expand the working knowledge with Cisco-Systems for everyone.[7]

Since there are various forms and ways of learning from customers, it is essential to be able to set up an appropriate form of learning for the given situation. The customer is thereby no longer merely a passive receiver, but he becomes a real stakeholder with whom data are interactively exchanged.

## Listening to the right customers

There is hardly any doubt that customers have become very important partners for the strategic behaviour of corporations and their innovative activities. However, in this regard it is also necessary to bear in mind that there is a problem with all the previously discussed forms of cooperation between corporations and customers, namely that it is primarily concentrated on experiences, on existing products or services, and therefore on improvements as supplements to what already exists.

A method that pays attention strictly to specially qualified customers in a more future-oriented way is the so-called the 'lead user' concept. Suitable customers, targeted and chosen by a special method, should be included in strategic and product innovation processes. In this way, one should be able to arrive at a balanced, innovative portfolio by combining traditional market research, learning based on experience, and the future-oriented lead user concept.

Such specially identified lead users are not simply the big customers or the long-standing, loyal ones. More often they are the prophetic and unconventional thinkers. One needs to pay attention to them. As practical examples prove, they can indeed make meaningful, radical and not merely marginal contributions. Corporations like Hilti, Nortel, 3M and Kellogg, as well as different manufacturers in the field of medical technology and semi-conductor technology, have been using the lead user concept successfully for many years.[8]

According to Herstatt, the reason that the emphasis is on the so-called lead users with special attributes, rather than long-time large customers, is based on the results of a study in the USA. In a broadly based and in-depth investigation of 21 corporations in the field of disk-drive operating systems (manufacturers of storage media, such as floppy and hard disk drives), the question investigated was why corporations, which were able to become technological leaders, suddenly no longer are in a position to achieve new breakthroughs and are then overtaken by 'newcomers'. The reason according to the study lies in the fact that large firms often and primarily want from their suppliers only adaptive innovation which allows them to improve the use of existing systems and procedures. Radical innovations are not encouraged, because they would involve higher switching costs for the customers. The loyal customer can also be caught up in existing ideas and be afraid of change. One speaks therefore of 'functional fixedness'. If a supplier orients itself along the lines of only conventional market research to develop products and services to meet the wishes of its long-time good customers, then it will systematically fall back in its attempts to recognize future needs, radical innovations and new markets.

## In search of lead users

Lead users are particularly progressive customers (users or buyers) who on the one hand are motivated for innovation, and on the other have the qualifications and core competences required for change.

Lead users are customers with new needs which will be marketable only in the future, and because of whom corporations remain innovative. In many ways, the concept of the lead user is in accordance with the idea of the customer as stakeholder, namely a valuable partner to be taken into account in the operational process of value creation. The marketing concept of CRM and lead user shows that the synergies between marketing and the stakeholder view can be put to use.

The perception of the customers as stakeholders can be summarized in the following motto:

**Customers are not only buyers who are served through sales and distribution. They are also to be regarded as true stakeholders, who are benefit receivers and also benefit providers.**

From a stakeholder perspective, the following questions need to be clarified:

1. Is the paramount importance of perceiving customers as strategic stakeholders recognized in my corporation, meaning it is not only preached but also practised in concrete ways?
2. Which categories of customers are to be distinguished so that a sufficiently differentiated picture emerges? What are the benefit and risk potentials of these customer segments?
3. Which learning forms and procedures are appropriate in dealing with customers? Are the possibilities for collaborative learning being put to full use?
4. Are there any typical lead users in my business who could contribute to my strategies and innovations?

## Notes

1  Oakley (2004), p. 12.
2  Yahoo! (2006).
3  Jaruzelski and Dehoff (2007), p. 71.
4  Jaruzelski and Dehoff (2007), p. 71.
5  IBM (2006).
6  Cassingham (2006).
7  Prahalad and Ramaswamy (2005), p. 7.
8  Herstatt *et al.* (2002).

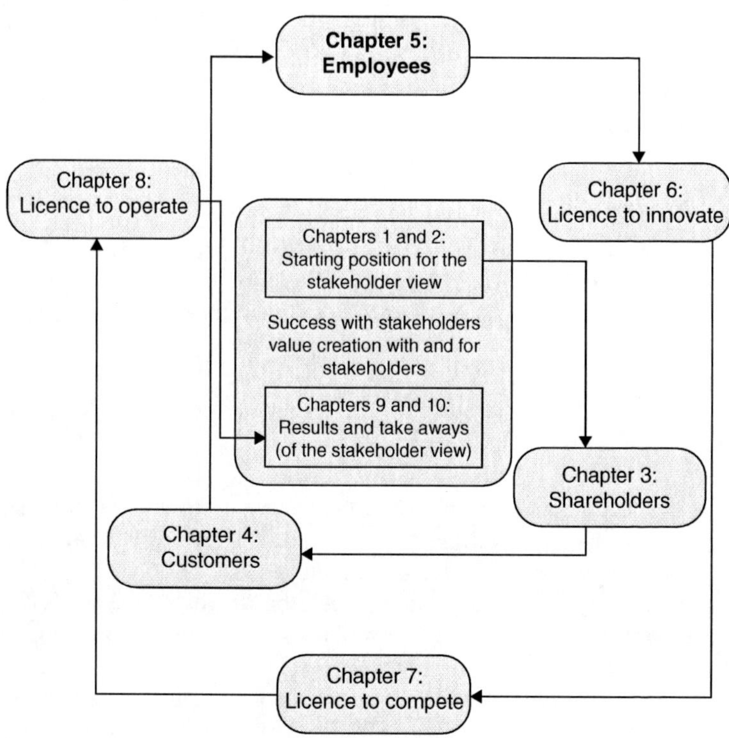

Chapter 5:
Employees
Chapter 8:
Licence to operate
Chapter 6:
Licence to innovate
Chapters 1 and 2:
Starting position for the
stakeholder view
Success with stakeholders
value creation with and for
stakeholders
Chapters 9 and 10:
Results and take aways
(of the stakeholder view)
Chapter 3:
Shareholders
Chapter 4:
Customers
Chapter 7:
Licence to compete

# 5
# Employees as knowledge partners

At present, a variety of aspects concerning the relationships of corporations to their employees are discussed. For example, the following story made the rounds on the Internet:

A human resources (HR) manager dies and goes to heaven. Because she is the first HR manager ever to do so, St Peter tells her, 'Whenever a new profession comes to heaven, the person has to spend a day in hell in order to choose where she or he would prefer to stay.' At first the manager protests and does not want to go along with this, but St Peter insists. So she takes the elevator down to hell. When the door opens she sees a beautiful golf course, where she soon meets a number of her former, deceased associates. The devil is extremely solicitous, and in the evening there is a marvellous dinner. Next day she takes the elevator back up to heaven and tells St Peter, 'I can't thank you enough for offering hell as an alternative. Please don't get me wrong, but I am going to take it It is so much like what I'm accustomed to.' St Peter smiles and says that he is not surprised. So she takes the elevator down to hell again. But this time when the door opens, she cannot believe her eyes. She sees an endless desert strewn with litter, and her colleagues dressed in rags collecting it. In the background, the devil is driving them with a shrill voice. Shocked she runs to him and asks what is going on and where the golf course is. 'Well, my dear, yesterday we were recruiting; today you are a member of staff.'

Surely no one intends to treat their employees quite like this. Our research showed that in many cases the importance of employees as stakeholders is valued highly (see Table 4.1, p. 67).

From the stakeholder perspective, a basic question for you to ask yourself is what categories of employees there are in your corporation. This is the first requirement for a differentiated interaction with these stakeholders, similar to the way we regarded shareholders and customers.

## The who is who of employees

Employees can be categorized by different criteria.[1] Some of these categories give some insight into possible stakeholder problems that can arise in a corporation.

### Hierarchical rank

From a stakeholder perspective, the difference between top managers and the rest of the employees has recently provided a lot of material for discussion due to the cases of horrendous increases in manager salaries. As John Bogle, a well-known US critic, says in a newspaper interview (*Tages-Anzeiger*, 2 April 2006),[2] based on the findings in his book:

> Let us compare the salaries of a top manager and a worker. Since 1980, the average salary of an employee has increased in real terms from USD 14,900 to only USD 15,900, the income of corporation heads from USD 625,000 to USD 4.5 million. I would say that there is a considerable difference between an increase of 7 percent and one of 614 percent. In the USA in the middle of the seventies, one percent of the richest people owned 18 percent of the national wealth; today they control 40 percent. Something like this is only comparable to the era of the robber barons at the beginning of the 20th century. And from that period we know that a society divided so crassly into haves and have-nots is headed for massive conflicts.

Due to the increasing discrepancy in salaries, there is fear of employees' lack of motivation or inner resignation, or even social conflict.

### Level of education

The increasing level of education of employees has strongly influenced their expectations of corporations. In some places, the benefits corporations are willing to extend to their employees have expanded accordingly. Here is a quote from one of our interviews:

> 'I think that dealing with employees respectfully is customary for us, whether it be agreeing on goals, hardship cases, recruitment. This is demonstrated by the fact that as far as I know we have never had any mass dismissals or anything similar. Solutions are sought for problems. The employees are not just simply left with a problem.'

Employees with a high level of education and specialized knowledge are increasingly drawn into ever more complex decision-making processes, receive more opportunities for continuing education, and have more freedom to determine their work than those poorly qualified.

## Job profile

The coming together of various job types in a corporation can lead to increased creativity. Innovative teams in a corporation are often made up of employees with different professional backgrounds and correspondingly different cultural experiences. This interdisciplinary quality challenges the group to seek commonality and differences in their points of view and methods of proceeding, and also to broaden their view as a result of the possibilities of their combined knowledge. Jack Welch, the CEO of General Electric, removed the borders between divisions in order to allow for problem solving by interdisciplinary teamwork. A study of various innovative programmes at Hewlett-Packard confirmed that interdisciplinary teams are more innovative than others. The reason lies in the fact that they have the necessary resources and abilities at their disposal within the team. For the purpose of developing new technologies, they have both broad as well as in-depth knowledge. Another example is Matsushita at the end of the 1980s, when they successfully put a bread-baking machine on the market. After early efforts had failed, Matsushita managed the breakthrough because organizational barriers had been dissolved and various project teams were able to work in an interdisciplinary way.

Interdisciplinary approaches, however, can also lead to cultural differences and tensions. We were able to observe actual trench warfare between different job types in our empirical inquiries. Needless to say, such situations have negative effects on the knowledge flow among the employees, and it is then not possible to use the potential of these stakeholders optimally.

### Domain affiliation

Observations similar to those in the interdisciplinary realm could be made regarding domain affiliation. Increased creativity is juxtaposed with the risk of conflict.

## The appeal of your company

The employees, as shown above, are mentioned together with the customers as the most important or strategic stakeholders of corporations. Accordingly, many corporations express the importance of their employees in their mission statement. Here is an excerpt from UBS's description of its core competence:

> Meritocracy: From each individual, we expect enterpreneurial thinking and initiative. We as a corporation want to recruit successfully the most highly qualified employees, and cultivate them in order to ensure lasting loyalty. Decisions regarding recognition, remuneration and career are made on the basis of achievement. We support our employees and invest in their development.

This quote demonstrates that employees are recognized as knowledge bearers, who determine the success of the corporation. As we have seen in various cases, it is essential for a corporation to make full use of this benefit potential. It is not sufficient for employees to be in a suitable business environment which permits and stimulates the development of their abilities; they also want to be accepted as true stakeholders. The decisive questions are how a corporation stimulates knowledge, and how it becomes an attractive employer.

A British survey of over 600 corporations investigated which factors are important for a corporation to be seen as an attractive employer. The main expectations of employees concern the following factors[3]:

- Work content
- Job security
- Loyalty
- Opportunities to take responsibility
- Opportunities to employ one's skills in a variety of ways.

According to the HR-Barometer,[4] Swiss corporations are generally seen as attractive employers, in fact a third of them as very attractive. From this, one can conclude that in many cases they have an appropriate recognition of the employees as stakeholders, and do not just regard them as production or cost factors. This is confirmed by statements of our interview partners:

'We found out in our climate report, a survey of employee satisfaction, that on average our material employment conditions are considered good. This was confirmed. There are other areas where people are less satisfied. But in any case they are satisfied with their salaries. And they recognize that we are strongly exposed to public opinion. I think that is logical in our business.'

Let us look at another example:

---

**Example: Swiss Re**
For a long time Swiss Re was considered to be an attractive employer, not only in the job market but also by its employees. The attention given to employee considerations in the past is impressive (e.g. investments in developing employees, incentive systems, employee-oriented culture, etc.). In this way, Swiss Re offered attractive work conditions for employees, thereby documenting the employees' acceptance as valuable stakeholders. Two specific shareholding programmes for employees can be given as examples: an employee shareholder plan and a share option plan. These programmes were intended to bring the interests of the employees and those of the shareholders closer together. However, the latest developments in Swiss Re (reducing jobs, for example) shows that attractive employee working conditions are always subject to change.

---

Also it is important for employees that their corporation has a good public image:

According to the Millennial Cause Study 2006 by Cone (USA), especially the birth years since 1979 pay attention to the reputation of

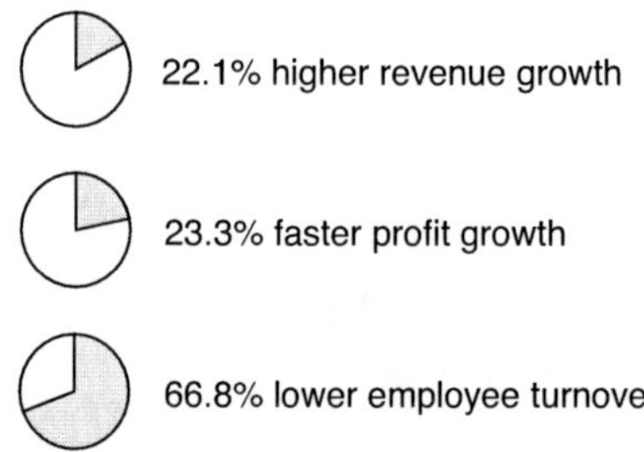


*Figure 5.1*   Performance when implementing all three HR measures
*Source*: Collins *et al.* (2006), p. 5.

the corporation when choosing an employer. Of those questioned, 79% said that they only wanted to work for an employer who took on social responsibility. Of those employed, 69% had informed themselves about the current engagement of their employer, and as a result 64% felt committed and behaved loyally toward the corporation. Also in Europe among well educated applicants, there is a clearly documented, steadily increasing demand that corporations adhere to social and ecological standards. This means that more than half of the job applicants look into the societal reputation and engagement of their potential employers.[5]

Several studies show that corporations which are attractive to their employees can achieve a higher performance. A study in the USA carried out among small businesses shows a positive connection between human resource management and corporation performance. The authors investigated the following criteria for effective HR management:

- Employee selection strategies (person-organization fit vs person-job fit).
- Employee management strategies (self-management vs controlling).
- Employee motivation and retention strategies (family environment vs individual monetary rewards).[6]

The results (see Figure 5.1 above) showed that the firms which implemented all three criteria had a significantly better performance than firms that implemented none of the three criteria.

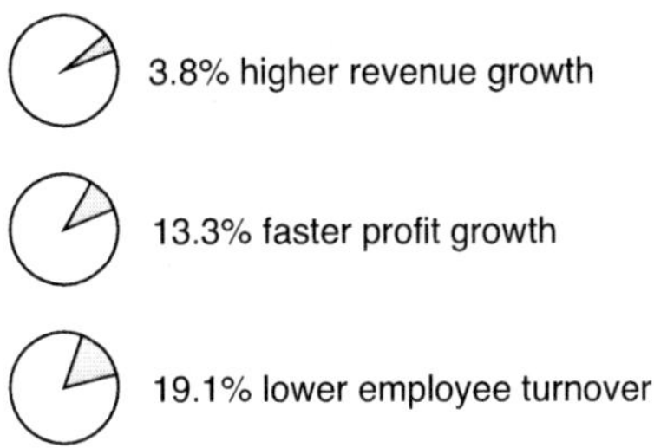


*Figure 5.2*   Performance when creating a family environment
*Source*: Based on Collins *et al.* (2006), p. 7.

Employees' motivation also has an important influence on the overall result, as the study of Collins *et al.* (2006) shows (see Figure 5.2).

## Employees at risk

Alongside the positive aspects mentioned, the work situation has become riskier for many employees in recent years.

> 'I think that the harder economic success is to achieve, the harder the procedures are internally in order not to disappoint the public. This means in many cases measures are taken at the expense of the employees.'

As soon as the economic situation becomes tense as was the case in 2002, then corporation employees are an important part of any cost-saving programme. The 2008–9 real estate crisis is already taking its toll on the financial sector. Citigroup, for example, is said to have cut approximately 13,000 jobs, UBS around 5500.[7] The diminishing marketability of employees becomes another important factor where there has been a pronounced specialization in function.

For corporations undergoing or planning strategic or structural changes, the insecurity and risks of the employees are plainly apparent. One of our interview partners expressed it in the following way:

> 'Not least of all was the shock for the stakeholders, especially the employees, when we suddenly had to reduce jobs. It was

completely unexpected, not because anyone promised that it wouldn't happen, but simply because no one could imagine it after the very emotional go-go-go build-up. We had to layoff two to three hundred people.'

Different studies point out the reasons for the increased negative effect of such risks.

## Poor internal communication

In some corporations, employees find out through rumours or the media that changes are being planned, and are inadequately informed by management. One such case was Orange Switzerland, a corporation we were investigating. One employee described the poor communication of the dismissals in the following way:

> 'An email was written to the employees: "The location in Bussigny will be kept." And the location was kept; but today it is only the seat of the technical division without one person who originally worked there.'

To overcome such frustrating communication problems, Orange later created an employee forum, a platform for a specific stakeholder dialogue:

> 'We realized that we had to include our employees more, and in fact in the preliminary stages of important decision making. We couldn't just confront them with *faits accomplis* but instead we had to include them early in the process. We learned that we needed an employee forum as a link between personnel and management, so that employees could be duly informed about changes affecting them, and that the concerns the personnel brought in could be taken into account.'

## Lack of trust

If management does not inform openly, then of course trust cannot be established. Often management does not take the concerns of the employees into account, because they are constantly being confronted by fresh challenges, such as the short life-cycle of products, falling prices and new regulations. Despite or because of the constant fight for success, there is no time for trust to be built up.

## Lack of motivation and continuing education

Employees have to be actively involved in changes and able to take responsibility. They also have to be allowed to learn from mistakes. In this way operational changes, IT solutions for example, can often lead to previous employee skills becoming obsolete and the employees having to prove their worth without the necessary skills in a new professional situation. This can lead to anxiety and insecurity. Continuing education should prepare employees for new corporation requirements.

Increasingly, the phenomenon of burnout is gaining importance. Many managers but also employees have the feeling of constantly working beyond their capacity. Their workload increases steadily without any corrective measures being taken. Important factors to consider in this regard are that structural changes are occurring more frequently, that contradictions between proclaimed and lived business principles exist, and that topics such as family policy, health and work–life balance are often only perceived as momentarily fashionable ideas and not taken seriously.

An EU-wide study shows that the main reasons for burnout are comparable for all of Europe:

- High requirements (quantitative, cognitive, emotional and sensory)
- Little control and little leeway in making decisions about what, how, when and how much to work
- No demanding work content
- Little possibility for personal and professional development at work and excessive supervision
- Lack of the necessary resources to complete the work
- Lack of support from colleagues and superiors
- Low level of remuneration
- Job insecurity as well as insecure working conditions[8]

Often additional factors are conflicts in the team or with the environment. These chronic stress situations can lead to illness and, on the other hand, to the fact that the individuals affected are generally less productive and particularly less creative. They are exposed to the risk of failing. This phenomenon should not be underestimated in knowledge-intensive fields.

With the acceleration of change in business and technology, job security is an especially important factor in the risk–benefit appraisal of employees, as the following quote of an interview partner makes clear:

> 'One has the advantage of having very good long-term employees, but one pays a price for giving people a certain amount of security. However, one cannot expect to have long-term and highly specialized employees, and at the same time not give them the assurance that when they are 50 one is not going to simply show them the door.
>
> So one either makes use of the market and takes people on when one needs them, and they work for money and leave after three years, or they commit themselves long-term and specialize and give up their marketability. This is the trade-off; this is the polarity we are in. It is one of our challenges.'

## Zero size

In many industries in recent years, an attitude has crystallized that the employees are the primary cost producers. One can find interesting examples of this in the telecommunications industry.

The importance of employees, who as civil servants of the Swiss postal and telephone system had had secure and privileged positions, changed at Swisscom in the course of the liberalization and partial privatization after 1998. The competition among the new telecom-providers demanded increased efficiency and job reduction. The same effects can be observed whenever liberalization and partial privatizing takes place, as a comparison with the telecom-privatizing in the countries of the EU shows (see Table 5.1).[9]

*Table 5.1*   Telecom privatization in Europe

| Country | Corporation | Time span | Number of redundancies and early retirements | In percent |
|---|---|---|---|---|
| Austria | Austrian Telecom | 1998–2003 | 1,850 | 10 |
| Denmark | Tele Danmark | 1997–1999 | 2,500 | unknown |
| Germany | German Telecom | 1995–1999 | over 50,000 | 20 |
| UK | British Telecom | 1984–1994 | 82,000 | 34 |

Manager communiqués can at times give the impression that perpetual cost reduction, and therefore job reduction, is the main purpose of the corporation. Cost reduction is now being described as a core competence! This can lead to grotesque exaggerations, which put a heavy strain on stakeholder relations.

An acquaintance working for such a 'streamlined' corporation commented dryly at lunch: 'We are so slim as the result of reducing our costs, that the next challenge will cause us to collapse completely.'

In particular, future opportunities cannot be taken advantage of without a sensible reserve cushion: in our investigations, we came upon corporations that had just had a radical restructuring behind them when the business cycle improved. The personnel potentials were so weak that they were not in a position to take advantage of the market opportunities.

Instead of relying solely on the 'zero-size phenomenon' of minimizing personnel costs with its two-sided effect, one should also think about how to put the employees' knowledge to use in order to increase the revenue side of the equation.

## Using the knowledge of employees

Especially in knowledge-intensive industries, which are particularly prevalent in industrialized countries, employees often make corporation-specific investments in their further education and knowledge development. An example of this can be seen at Swiss Re, as an interview partner impressively stated:

'We are a corporation with a large number of well educated specialists, who not only have academic degrees but also a great deal of professional experience in their field. Among them are engineers, climate experts, physicians, etc. For example, we have our own medical department for determining mortality risks. It is really a great "trick box". These employees have to be able to work together, and they have to be able to understand new developments. They need to educate themselves for the long-term, and at the same time they have to further the education of our clients.'

In such a situation it is particularly important to establish a partnership relationship with the employees, since otherwise cases of demotivation and inner resignation can mean especially high losses in the productivity of the corporation.

In order that employees are willing on a long-term basis to expand their knowledge and to place it at the disposal of a corporation, it is important to cultivate employee willingness and disposition. This can happen by including the employees in the decision making and the information flow of the corporation.[10] According to the HR-Barometer, this is true for 40 per cent of the employees in Switzerland. A further possibility is the remuneration for special achievements of employees in the area of knowledge management.

In this regard, good relationships to employee organizations are also effective, as an interview partner confirms:

> 'Our corporation has cultivated a long tradition of open and constructive partnership. The primary goal is maintaining good work relations. To this end, a permanent dialogue is necessary with the employee organizations.'

In contrast to many other European countries, where work conflicts are often carried out between the corporations and the unions, Switzerland has a long tradition of fruitful cooperation called social partnership. An interview partner confirms this:

> 'I am convinced that the social partnership in Switzerland is one of the factors making it an attractive location, even though unions still play an important role in the game of work relations. I have no use for solutions that seek to exclude the unions from collective procedures. This partner is part of the power game. I think, with this policy we are following now, we are able to be more credible in our employee relations. Nonetheless, I can't verify it quantitatively.'

A British study shows the importance of a psychological contract with employees in order to strengthen their commitment.[11] This is to be done by cultivating a good relationship to the stakeholder 'co-workers' actively and consciously, in order to keep and continue to strengthen them.

An impressive example of how the knowledge of the employees can be used even in large corporations was recently described in the press.

It is interesting that in addition to the employees a further circle of
stakeholders was drawn in:

> The world's largest information technology corporation (IBM) reg-
> ularly holds innovation jam sessions. It is a kind of on-line brain-
> storming in which the 329,000 employees have the opportunity
> via Intranet to discuss, exchange ideas and develop projects. For
> the most recent occasion, IBM expanded the circle by inviting cus-
> tomers, suppliers, universities and the families of employees to the
> jam session. 150,000 people from 104 countries participated and
> produced 46,000 ideas. In Europe, the Swiss were the third most
> active participant after the British and the Germans.[12]

### Kinds of knowledge

Basically, there are two kinds of knowledge which can be distinguished from each other: explicit and tacit. Explicit knowledge can
be easily formalized and shared, for example in the form of texts,
instructions and formulas. In contrast, tacit knowledge is hidden and
not as easily accessible. It depends on experience and perception, and
is therefore bound to the individual. For example, it includes acquired
manual abilities of which an individual is often not even conscious.
For this reason, tacit knowledge is difficult to put in writing. It can,
however, be handed on, as for example when a master craftsman initi-
ates an apprentice into a trade, and teaches the tricks and trade secrets
which are not in the textbooks. This is similarly true for other activities, in which knowledge or talent that is difficult to grasp plays an
important part. For the purpose of goal-directed use, one needs to
clarify what kind of knowledge is at stake in the case of important
employees. Knowledge management is able to then build on this. In
the corporations we investigated, there was usually no professional
knowledge management. The following quote expresses this:

> 'All right, if you are addressing knowledge management, it is true
> that we buried various attempts after a certain amount of effort. At
> present, it is true that we have no knowledge management as such.
> And in some of the group associates, we also don't have any sys-
> tematic, which is to say well-supported, knowledge management.
> This certainly isn't good nor good enough in the long run.'

This means that the knowledge which employees could make available and its value-creation potential are not being fully used.

## Refining knowledge

For a corporation, it is important to be able to rely on not merely the *explicit* knowledge of its employees, because this knowledge is generally easy to access and will unfortunately be available to the competition sooner or later. Therefore, the corporation needs to try to tap the tacit knowledge of its employees and disseminate it internally, thereby improving its competitive position.

In the knowledge-management concept of the Japanese scientists Nonaka and Takeuchi,[13] four steps show how you can first transform tacit into explicit knowledge, how the explicit knowledge is enriched in order to create new knowledge, and how this knowledge through practice is finally transformed into tacit knowledge. These four steps are called socialization, externalization, combination and internalization:

1. *Socialization*: Tacit knowledge and common theoretical models are created. This happens in that the employees complete common tasks; and by observing each other, they learn from each other. It is a learning-by-doing process, like the above example of the master craftsman and the apprentice.
2. *Externalization*: The purpose is to extract the tacit knowledge which the employees have gained, so that it can later be made available to everyone. This happens in dialogues and discussions. Problems and their solutions can, for example, be presented by using metaphors, analogies, concepts, hypotheses or visualizations, and thereby made available. By discussing their various ideas and comparing them with each other, the employees get to know the different points of view and considerations of their colleagues better, and at the same time are made aware of the similarities or contradictions in the individual concepts and theoretical models.
3. *Combination*: The employees transfer the metaphors, visualizations and concepts, which they worked out in the previous step, into a system of knowledge. This means that the results of the discussion are put down in written form and made available to everyone, either in the form of documents or databases. In addition, the employees have to connect these newly gained insights with existing knowledge in the corporation so as to generate new knowledge.
4. *Internalization*: The newly acquired knowledge is broadened and applied. Through a process of trial-and-error the employees have to find out whether their new concepts and hypotheses function in practice and adjust them accordingly. In this way, tacit knowledge comes about and closes the circle.

Under ideal circumstances, these four steps are being repeated constantly, so that a knowledge spiral emerges in which knowledge is continuously expanding. At the same time, more and more employees are being drawn into the process, by which knowledge is dispersed throughout the whole corporation. This concept of knowledge management takes into account our concern to regard the employees as stakeholders, and to encourage and use their knowledge potential.

Assuring knowledge transfer is an important concern of ABB. Within the next 10 years, almost 20 per cent of the personnel of ABB Germany will be retired, and by the year 2026 it will be as much as 53 per cent. For this reason, it is of utmost importance for ABB to keep as much of the available knowledge as possible within the firm. The corporation has therefore introduced project 'Generations', in which a young and an older ABB employee head a project together in order to assure the transfer of knowledge.[14]

The consideration of employee stakeholders has led us to the following motto:

**Employees should first of all be seen as knowledge bearers crucial for corporate success, and not as a mass to be manipulated in order to reduce costs.**

From a stakeholder perspective ask yourself the following questions:

1. What personnel categories are decisive for the strategic success of my corporation?
2. What are the benefit and risk potentials of my various personnel categories?
3. How do I see the employee potential in the context of today's strongly propagated cost reduction? To what extent am I willing to withstand this pressure or even make long-term investments in the knowledge potential of my employees?
4. How favourable are the conditions in my corporation for using, disseminating and encouraging the knowledge of my employees? Where are unexploited pockets of knowledge?

### Other important core stakeholders

In the last three chapters, we have discussed the importance of the generally recognized strategically relevant stakeholders: namely the shareholders, customers and employees, the so-called magic triangle. According to the situation in which a corporation finds itself or according to the industry, other stakeholders can of course be strategically relevant. These stakeholders are to be regarded similarly to those of the magic triangle.

In the case of the liberalization of the telecom industry in many countries in recent years, the regulators were stakeholders of great strategic importance.

For firms in the pharmaceutical industry, HMO organizations or health care insurers may be strategic stakeholders and in countries with strong state influences on the economy, the governments and their agencies are of top relevance. This was confirmed by our empirical investigations.

Other stakeholders are the media and NGOs. However, the media generally have not been ranked among the top ten stakeholders. Nevertheless, one of our interview partners made the following statement:

'I was in Canada when Vioxx, one of the major medicines of Merck, was withdrawn from the market. The news was picked up by the media, and they began to communicate information they had picked up here and there. It was a big mess. Merck had to answer lots and lots of questions from their patients, for which they didn't have all the answers. For the first time in many years, we realized the power of the media in the pharmaceutical industry... We are working on this, because I think that you need to have a good understanding of the dynamics involved. I'm not sure that we understand the dynamics exactly.'

Although many companies do have Public Relations or Media Relations departments, knowledge regarding the media remains isolated in these departments and is hardly integrated into strategic management. The media are perceived as a perilous black box that follow their own, often profit-driven rules and defy management control.

Other stakeholders closely linked to the media are NGOs. NGOs often use publicity and the media to get attention from the public and exert pressure on companies. However, NGOs are perceived not only as risky stakeholders but also as potential partners to share knowledge

*Table 5.2*   Importance of stakeholders by industry

| Stakeholders/industry (ranking) | Telco | FS | Total |
| --- | --- | --- | --- |
| Customers | 1 | 1 | 1 |
| Employees | 2 | 2 | 2 |
| Shareholders, investors, owners | 3 | 3 | 3 |
| Society | 5 | 4 | 4 |
| Regulators | 4 | 7 | 5 |
| Business partners | 6 | 6 | 6 |
| Government | 7 | 5 | 7 |
| Suppliers | 10 | 9 | 8 |
| Politicians | 9 | 10 | 9 |

and to build partnerships regarding societal issues. At Swiss Re, one of our partners thinks NGOs will become one of the most important stakeholders in his business in the coming years:

> 'I see the potential for change primarily with the unconventional stakeholders, to which the NGOs clearly belong. There is a lot of movement there. This area is becoming more and more important for us.'

In Table 5.2 we see which stakeholders were mentioned and ranked by the firms we analysed in the telecom (Telco) and financial services (FS) industries according to their importance (frequency).

In the next three chapters, we will look at the influence of stakeholders on strategic development.

## Notes

1  Grote and Staffelbach (2006).
2  For more details see Bogle (2005).
3  Guest *et al.* (2003), p. 298ff.
4  Grote and Staffelbach (2006).
5  Collins *et al.* (2006).
6  Collins *et al.* (2006), p. 4.
7  Manager-Magazin.de (2008), Bartz (2008).
8  EIRO (2001a).
9  EIRO (1999).

10  Cf. the British study by Sturgess *et al.* (2001).
11  Sturgess *et al.* (2003).
12  Neue Zürcher Zeitung (NZZ) (2006), p. 37.
13  Nonaka and Takeuchi (1995).
14  ABB (2007).

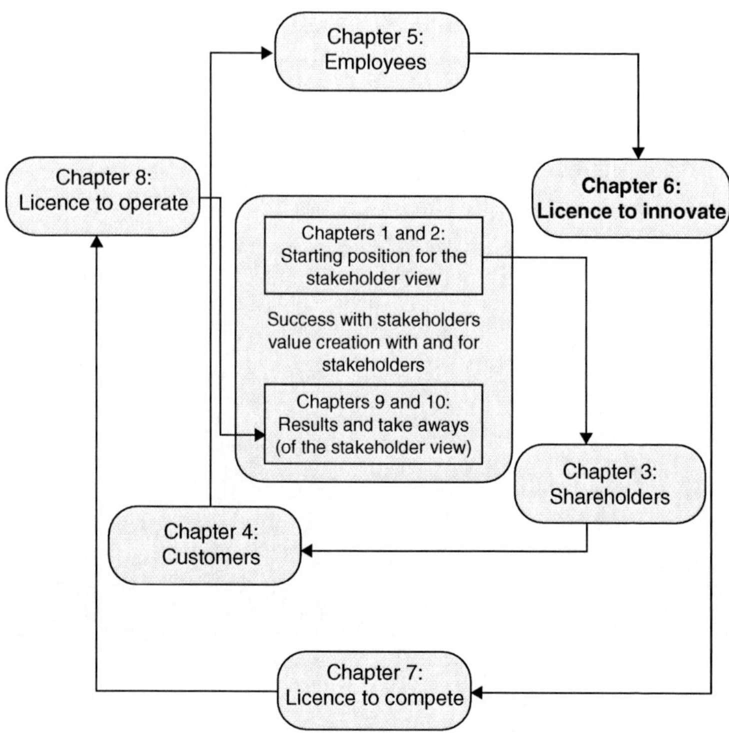

Chapter 5:
Employees

Chapter 8:
Licence to operate

Chapter 6:
Licence to innovate

Chapters 1 and 2:
Starting position for the
stakeholder view

Success with stakeholders
value creation with and for
stakeholders

Chapters 9 and 10:
Results and take aways
(of the stakeholder view)

Chapter 3:
Shareholders

Chapter 4:
Customers

Chapter 7:
Licence to compete

# 6
# The strategic core of your stakeholders

If one compares the strategic management of similar corporations, like Coca-Cola and PepsiCo, for example, then one may ask oneself why the two corporations achieve completely different results. This is the key question of modern strategic management.

The rivalry between Coca-Cola and PepsiCo is over a hundred years old. For years Coca-Cola was the undisputed leader, while Pepsi limped behind in turnover and in share price. A few years ago Pepsi changed its strategy, because it realized that it could not win the 'Cola-War', and diversified. Pepsi now sells mineral water (Aquafina) and sports drinks (Gatorade), and has moved ahead of its rival for the first time in its history. In the meantime, Coca-Cola is also selling mineral water (Dasani) and sports drinks (Powerade), but the sales figures are clearly behind those of Pepsi. Aquafina is the most sold mineral water, and Gatorade dominates the sports drink market with a share of 80%. Coca-Cola has made it to 15 per cent only in the last five years. During this time Pepsi developed in accordance with customer taste, and this is not the end of the story: Pepsi's greatest strength is not in the area of beverages but in snacks, where together with Frito-Lay it controls 60 per cent of the US snack-market. Coca-Cola has nothing to counter it with. Today Pepsi has become a food product multinational, while Coca-Cola has remained a beverage producer.[1]

According to the economic model, competition should erode the difference in the results, in this case the strategic rent. Business reality, however, has shown that this is not necessarily so, and that corporations often retain their different results over long periods of time.

Different contextual conditions for the individual competitors, such as divergent economic positions, market conditions, locations, etc., can explain the difference in strategic results. Under similar environmental conditions, such as with Coca-Cola and PepsiCo, the different results are primarily based on the fact that managers and employees are in a situation of bounded rationality. They therefore interpret similar situations differently, and respond accordingly with different strategies. Different strategic behaviour leads to different competitive positions and finally to strategic differences in the outcome, which can often continue over a long period of time. Because situations as well as the people in a corporation change, this causes further differences in the way a corporation behaves, leading again to differences in results.

In order to explain differences in strategic outcomes, two lines of argumentation have developed in traditional strategic theories in response to the question below.

## Strategic success explained

In the market-based view of strategy (often also called the industry structure view), the first line of argumentation distinguishes two factors in strategic results, namely the attractiveness of the industry's structures and the corporation's own strategic behaviour.

In order to determine market attractiveness, which is to say the first factor, five influential aspects need particular consideration, namely the incumbent competitors, the possible market entry of new competitors, the power of suppliers and buyers, and the effect of substitute products. Therefore, on the basis of the knowledge of these influential aspects, the goal is to find an area with as little competition as possible, and thereby a position in which a so-called quasi-monopolistic rent is possible. From this point of view, in order for a corporation to be strategically successful, it has to be able to take up a sustainable and defendable position in attractive, which is to say less competitive, markets or niches. It is then in a particularly strong position in relation to its competitors and customers.[2]

The resource-based view of strategy, the second line of argumentation, is based on the fact that usually there is a limited supply of resources, and that therefore among corporations there is both

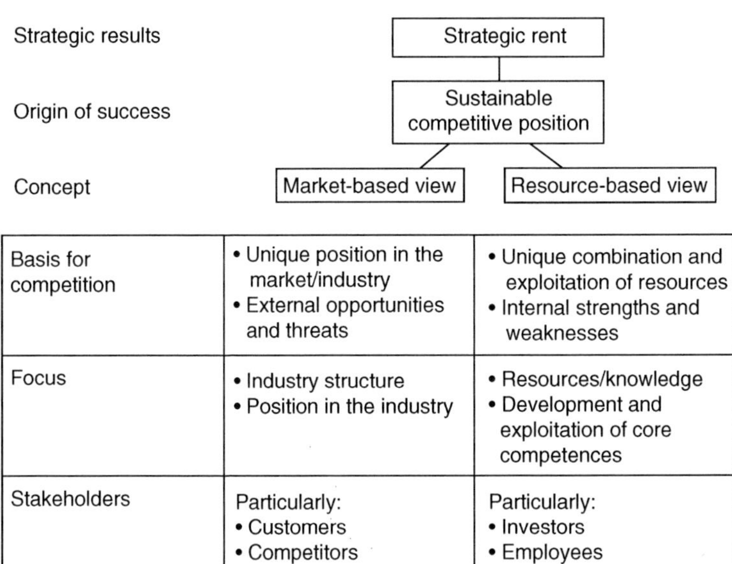


| | Market-based view | Resource-based view |
|---|---|---|
| Basis for competition | • Unique position in the market/industry<br>• External opportunities and threats | • Unique combination and exploitation of resources<br>• Internal strengths and weaknesses |
| Focus | • Industry structure<br>• Position in the industry | • Resources/knowledge<br>• Development and exploitation of core competences |
| Stakeholders | Particularly:<br>• Customers<br>• Competitors | Particularly:<br>• Investors<br>• Employees |

*Figure 6.1*   The market- and resource-oriented view

unequal access to and disposition of resources. For a sustainable and defensible position, it is decisive that one has the best possible access to specific strategically relevant resources, such as capital or knowledge, in order to develop a competitive advantage. These resources once acquired have to be exploited as systematically as possible. Figure 6.1 compares these two lines of argument.

In both approaches, the importance of special stakeholder groups comes to the fore. In the market view, it is the customers and competitors; in the resource view, the investors and employees. However, neither approach systematically identifies or uses all the strategically relevant stakeholders, as already discussed in Chapter 2.

In this chapter we therefore want to correct this shortcoming by first looking at all the stakeholders as possible sources for strategically relevant resources, before we look at positioning in the stakeholder network in the next chapter.

## Race for resources

In our investigation, we were able see that there is often an astonishing difference of opinion within a managerial team as to which
core competences a corporation's success are based on. One manager
openly admitted the following in discussion with us:

> 'You will also notice that I too find it hard to name our core
> competences one, two, three.'

And even in cases where there is more or less a common understanding about core competences, there is a lack of awareness about what
contribution the various stakeholders have made to the results. In
this regard, we noticed areas of tension of strategic importance in
practically each one of the investigated cases.

Empirical studies show that the reason some corporations have the
best competitive results is because of intangible resources which set
them apart from their competitors, and thereby give them a sustainable and defendable competitive position. The more intangible the
resources of a corporation are, the more difficult they are to imitate,
and the greater their contribution to competitive advantage.

One study[3] of small and medium-sized corporations in Austria
showed that in this view the continuing education and the motivation of employees were of decisive importance. These factors are
a determining factor for the profits and the earnings of small and
medium-sized corporations.

In another more comprehensive study, the important intangible
resources of British corporations were identified:

- Intellectual property rights of patents, trademarks, copyright and
  registered designs
- Trade secrets
- Contracts and licences
- Databases
- Information in the public domain
- Personnel and organizational networks
- Know-how of employees, professional advisers, suppliers and
  distributors
- Reputation of products and corporation

- Culture of the organization, e.g. the ability of the organization to react to challenge, to cope with change, etc.[4]

Corporation and product reputation, employee know-how and organizational networks were primarily shown to be most important for success.

The focus on intangible resources does not exclude the fact that tangible resources are also important, such as plant and technical solutions, as components of core competences. These, however, are often easier for the competition to imitate than the intangible resources such as knowledge, and often have a less long-term effect, as the following quote from an interview partner from the telecommunications industry confirms:

> 'And that [service] is today still one of the central points for us, when one realizes that in regard to the technology all the competitors are very similar. All three operators apply the same technology. As soon as a manufacturer develops some new technology, all three competitors can buy it. Where is there a chance to differentiate?'

For this reason the focus is on the intangible resources.

## Intangible resources

Our experience and our studies of corporations clearly show that stakeholder relations are an important source of intangible resources. However, it is also noticeable (as already mentioned in Chapter 5) that these sources are rarely systematically put to use. With the customers in mind, one of our interviewees said the following:

> 'The problem is that we do not always utilize the knowledge of our customers systematically. Although we make inquiries, we do so usually somewhat haphazardly. We don't fill in the gaps in what we know. Sometimes if we need to know something, we go to the customers and the markets to get the knowledge we need. However, I still think that we don't put this knowledge to use well enough.'

On the basis of the resource contributions from stakeholder relations, a corporation can develop core competences that enable it to develop

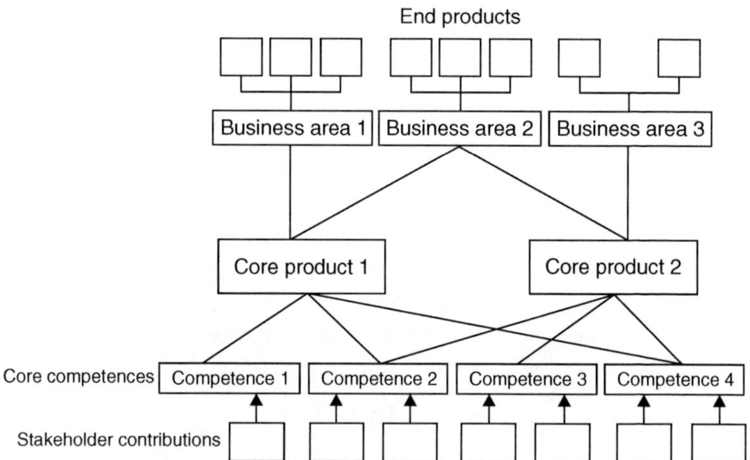


*Figure 6.2*  Stakeholder contributions to core competences
*Source*: Figure based on Prahalad and Hamel (1990), p. 81. Reprinted by permission of *Harvard Business Review*, from 'The Core Competence of the Corporation' by C. K. Prahalad and G. Hamel, May–June 1990. Copyright © 1990 by the Harvard Business School Publishing Corporation; all rights reserved.

core products or services, which are then offered by various business units as end products or end services. This logic is represented in a diagram taken from Prahalad and Hamel, in Figure 6.2.

## Stakeholder contribution

If you look more closely, as discussed above, at the possible contributions stakeholders can make so that your corporation is in a sustainable and defensible competitive position, you will see that there are various possibilities:

### Information/Knowledge

In Chapters 3 (Shareholders), 4 (Customers) and 5 (Employees), we have referred to the fact that stakeholders have access to important information. This can be systematically evaluated, as the following makes clear:

'The feedback we receive by email, telephone, letter is collected and fed into product development. In the future, we want to attain this information more professionally. I see greater opportunities to go beyond our competitors in knowledge management.'

## Emotionality

On the basis of their specific values, stakeholders can often make a contribution to the emotionality of a corporation and its brand. With very technological corporations or with corporations confronted with different local cultures, it can be very important that on this basis the products or services are emotionally compatible. Here is the comment of an interviewee:

> 'We are part of an international shareholder package that includes 110 countries and 280,000 people. On the other hand, we are also very local, an emotional brand which acts independently locally. Maintaining the balance can be very demanding.'

The broad relationship network to the shareholders of this corporation is promising, on the one hand. On the other, the local orientation can also be seen as a positive element.

## Experience

Stakeholders, especially the customers, may have basic experience in connection with the products or with the markets (see also Chapter 4). The corporations we investigated confirmed this again and again. This is in agreement with earlier findings, that customers are the most important stakeholders.

> 'Naturally we have a great many interactions with our customers. As you know, customers often have the advantage of seeing details better ... We certainly have the advantage of having a broader perspective, since we are in direct contact with so many customers. We can absorb the experience of ten different customers, from ten different perspectives. This way, we can also focus more on the details.'

## Credibility/trust

Open and long-term relationships to stakeholders can strengthen the credibility of a corporation in interaction with all types of business partner regarding products or marketing. A whole range of new studies has shown that trust between business partners can support positive outcomes in the long run. In addition, acceptance is built up among the employees, the customers and the public. This is confirmed by the following quote from an interview partner:

> 'We are a corporation that had to reduce jobs. We probably have by far the most expensive social compensation plan of any corporation in Switzerland. I am convinced, however, that we have to have this for two reasons. If due to an effort on our part we are able to mediate new prospects for the people who have to leave, then we foster acceptance in the long run and a loyalty bonus from the employees who remain. Second, it is the social and economic obligation of a successful corporation not to create unemployment but to find solutions.'

### Image/Reputation

Stakeholders can boost the image of a corporation or individual products and services. We know that banks analyse the image of their customers when granting loans. Good relations between a credit-seeker and its stakeholders are rated positively. As we have seen on the list of intangible resources (compare p. 102), there is great potential in a good reputation for building up a sustainable, defensible competitive advantage.

### Core values

Stakeholders can contribute important new core values. On the one hand, they may belong to other social networks that have their own value systems. On the other, they have their own experience in dealing with values. Today various pharmaceutical corporations are faced with the necessity of having to position themselves anew. The core values of stakeholders such as physicians, customers or health insurance companies play a central role in this.

### Transparency

Fostering relations with the various stakeholder groups can increase transparency. This in turn creates trust as well as direct advantages in business transactions.

> 'In earlier times, we communicated much less. Our financial statement was published once a year. A lot has changed now. I believe

that communication has changed for the better in relation to investors, institutional investors and our customers. We are more transparent in presenting who we are and what we do.'

Previously we saw how stakeholder relations can result in resource advantages for a corporation. However, it is also possible that these stakeholder resources bring about not only benefits in a corporate value creation process, but also risks. It is possible that the experience of certain stakeholder groups may prove to be unimportant or stakeholders might intentionally pass on false information. In any case, you should always check the credibility of stakeholders as sources of strategically relevant resources.

## Stakeholders as sources of resources

As already mentioned, seemingly beneficial stakeholder interactions can turn out to bear risks. This danger exists if one does not know the stakeholder well, or has only had short or sporadic contact. This means that no real relationship could be established to enhance mutual trust and clarify possible misunderstandings; the latter arising perhaps due to a lack of information or to a difference in values.

In our study of corporations, we observed the following relationship patterns with various outcomes:

- Solely informational relationships

In this type of relationship, the corporation and the respective stakeholder groups merely exchange information based on their knowledge, experience, core values, etc. This makes sense if enlarging the information basis is a resource sufficient for developing a core competence. The danger in doing so is that the quality of the stakeholders' information may not be adequately appraised, except in the cases where the stakeholder group is a recognized expert in the field. The advantage of this relationship pattern is that it is not very time-consuming, and can often be maintained on the basis of periodic and routine evaluations (e.g. lead user questionnaires).

- Communication relationships

In this type of relationship pattern, an intensive communication process takes place while exchanging strategically relevant resources.

There has to be a need to explain things on the part of the corporation and/or the relevant stakeholder groups so that a transfer of resources can take place. For the corporation, the advantage of this relationship pattern lies in the fact that the danger of misunderstandings, but also the failure to recognize the quality of the stakeholder, is less likely than in the information relationship. The disadvantage is that in addition to being more time-consuming, either the corporation can dominate the stakeholder group or vice versa, namely the stakeholder group can dominate the corporation in the communication process. Both can lead to either dependency or one-sidedness.

- Learning relationships

If on the side of the corporation, as well as on the side of the respective stakeholder group, the need arises to search for innovative solutions for common problems by bringing together their various resources, then this complex and time-consuming relationship pattern is the right one. The advantage is that via the learning process both sides can develop new innovative competences, which could not have been achieved alone and which are difficult for the competition to imitate. It becomes problematic if either the corporation or the affected stakeholder is not willing to proceed in a partner-like manner, or when one partner seeks a one-sided advantage. In this case, learning processes are not possible for either side.

In each concrete case, it is up to you to decide which relationship type is appropriate with each specific stakeholder.

## Trading core competences?

You can recognize core competences with authentic and long-term effectiveness by the four characteristics that follow:[5]

- Creating additional benefit for the customer

Core competences must clearly create added value for the products or services in ways that can be seen, appreciated and sought by the customers. By bringing in sources of information or the resources of strategically relevant stakeholders, there is less danger of taking a purely internally oriented view in the development of products or services.

- Scarcity

Core competence should be built on the scarcity of resources, so that access is difficult for your competitors. In this regard, especially those stakeholders are of interest for whom specific resources are available. Due to a highly specific resource, the market or trade is limited, and therefore competition has not been able to establish itself. Here the intangible resources already mentioned, for which stakeholders can be important sources, play a decisive role.

- Not substitutable

The resources which the respective stakeholder groups have to contribute should not be replaceable by any other resources, because otherwise the core competence can easily be substituted.

- Not imitable

The core competence should not be imitable, in that the combination of secret resources of which the core competence consists is not clearly recognizable. The implicit knowledge of the stakeholders, such as that of their employees, can be an important factor (see Chapter 5). An inimitable core competence also comes about when the access to resources is only possible on the basis of the specific developmental history in the relationship between the stakeholder groups and the corporation (path dependence).

## The 'Licence to Innovate'

The resource-based view of strategy is, as we have seen, connected to the fact that resources are usually limited and unequally distributed, and that resource asymmetries exist among corporations which can be used systematically. Therefore for a sustainable, defensible position it is decisive that one has access to specific, strategically relevant resources, such as capital and primarily knowledge, with which to develop unique core competences. These are hard for the competition to imitate and are therefore the basis for long-term success. Traditionally, this view considers the special value of investors (capital) and employees (knowledge) as decisive resources.[6] Through the

MY JOB
is SO CONFIDENTIAL
THAT I DON'T ACTUALLY KNOW
WHAT I DO!

systematic and early inclusion of all the strategic resources of the stakeholders, the corporation is not solely dependent on the subsequent answer of the market or society regarding its goods and services. It has already included the perspectives and resources of its strategically relevant stakeholders, while developing its products and services, as well as its basic core competences. This not only lessens the danger of painful and expensive adjustments later on, but strengthens chances for 'first mover advantage'. Under the aspect of core competences, the stakeholders that contribute important resources will be seen as the supporters of a sustainable competitive advantage. The cooperation with these stakeholders enables the corporation to make essential innovations; they help them to acquire a 'Licence to Innovate'.

> **Example: Nestlé (Swiss nutrition corporation)**
> In 2008, Nestlé announced that it will build a 'Chocolate
> Centre of Excellence' to develop premium quality chocolate.
> To improve its core competences to do this, it also included
> resources from external stakeholders: 'Thirty specialists from
> the confectionery, flavour and packaging branches [were to]
> develop marketable products for Nestlé brands like Cailler,
> Perugina, Baci or Nestlé Nori. They were not to depend on the
> corporation's own know-how alone, but were to include
> consultations with internationally known confectioneries,
> such as the top Belgian chocolate maker Pierre Marcolini for
> example.'[7]

Our discussion in this chapter allows us to conclude with the following motto:

**Stakeholder relationships can lead to unique core compe-
tences, and thereby provide your corporation with a basis
for acquiring a 'Licence to Innovate'.**

Ask yourself the following questions:

1. What are the core competences of my corporation today and in
   the future?
2. Which strategic resources are especially relevant for acquiring my
   'Licence to Innovate'?
3. Which of my stakeholders have the resources I need?
4. How can I establish a relationship to these stakeholders?

## Notes

1 Brooker (2006).
2 Porter (1985, 1998).
3 Leitner (2001).
4 Hall (1992, 1993).
5 Barney (1991).
6 i.e. Barney (1991); Grant (1996); Mahoney and Pandian (1992); Teece *et al.*
  (1997).
7 Locke (2002).

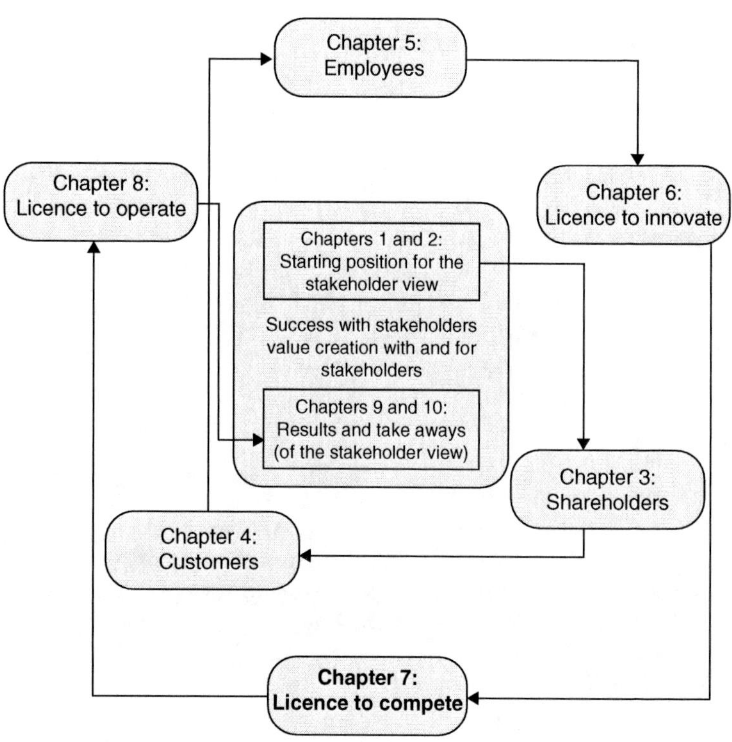

Chapter 5:
Employees
Chapter 8:
Licence to operate
Chapter 6:
Licence to innovate
Chapters 1 and 2:
Starting position for the
stakeholder view
Success with stakeholders
value creation with and for
stakeholders
Chapters 9 and 10:
Results and take aways
(of the stakeholder view)
Chapter 3:
Shareholders
Chapter 4:
Customers
Chapter 7:
Licence to compete

# 7
# The spider in the web

On the basis of the previous chapter, you are in a position to know who your stakeholders are. We have already discussed where the benefit and risk potentials in the stakeholder relationship may be found. However, we have not dealt with the fact that stakeholders are not only in contact with your corporation, but that they also have relationships among themselves. Although this is not surprising, our studies show that at present relatively few corporations concern themselves with networking. After a closer look, they are therefore often surprised at the effects such indirect relations can have on their own value-creation processes. Let us look at the following example:

---

**Example: Nike (the US sporting goods manufacturer)**
In the 1990s Nike was faced with calls to boycott its products. The reason was infringements against employee regulations in Asia, where Nike had subcontractors producing their goods.

At the beginning of the 1990s, NGOs (non-governmental organizations) and other activists were attracting attention to the work conditions in the factories in Indonesia supplying Nike. Violations of human and labour rights were widespread.

In 1996 *Life* magazine published a report about child labour in Sialkot (Pakistan). One of the pictures was of a 12-year-old boy sewing a Nike football. Consumer groups, unions and NGOs called for a boycott of Nike footballs produced in Sialkot.

---

At the end of 1997, Ernst & Young carried out an audit of a Korean subcontractor of Nike. In the report, Ernst & Young pointed out the serious health and safety hazards in the factory. The report was published by the *New York Times* and other newspapers.

Nike was confronted by a number of negative headlines badly damaging its image. Consumers and NGOs called for boycotts, people demonstrated in front of Nike stores and anti-Nike websites appeared on the internet, which still provide information on Nike[1] activities.

The negative details spread through Nike's whole stakeholder network thereby strengthening the effect of the demonstrators.


## Networking

The effects, which stakeholder networks and their neglect can have, are demonstrated by the impressive story of Shell's plans to sink Brent Spar in 1995.

**Example: Shell (Dutch-British oil and gas corporation)**
Until 1995 Shell was considered to be a very efficiently run oil corporation, possessing a great deal of technological expertise and a great deal of awareness of its responsibility concerning the environment and also of the legal situations in various countries.

This positive image suffered severely suddenly, when Shell decided to sink the oil platform Brent Spar into the North Sea. Let us take a closer look at this difficult situation for Shell from a network perspective.

After careful analysis of the various disposal possibilities, and after clarifying the legal, technological, economic and environmental restrictions, in addition to bilateral negotiations with the relevant national stakeholders, Shell UK decided on the plan of sinking the oil platform into the North Sea. However, none of the approximately 30 studies consulted were done by environmental specialists; instead all the studies were by experts with excellent credentials for technical off-shore solutions.

On the basis of its investigations, Shell had in no way expected the massive reaction that resulted from its decision. In addition to direct action, Greenpeace and other activists all over Europe, but especially in Germany, called for a consumer boycott. This boycott was supported by well-known politicians, among them Helmut Kohl the German Chancellor at the time. A whole network of stakeholders began to react interactively in addition to the consumers. As a result, Shell's turnover dropped significantly. In the course of the highly emotional debate over the Brent Spar platform, Shell gas stations were threatened with over thirty threats of arson, three of which were actually carried out. In this way, indirect effects in Shell's stakeholder network were triggered. Shell no longer knew what was going on and had no control over what was happening.

Greenpeace occupied Brent Spar a number of times, causing Shell to attempt to rid itself of the unwelcome guests by using water guns. The reactions of Shell UK were sporadic and for a long time Shell failed to recognize that Brent Spar was more than a national matter limited to Great Britain. Shell insisted on the fact that sinking the oil platform in the deep sea was the best solution, but failed to communicate why it had come to this conclusion in not releasing the experts' reports. On the whole, its communication policy was incomplete and outdated. Greenpeace, on the other hand, began a very effective media campaign in order to make its concerns known in Europe, and to activate a broad network of institutional opposition to Shell. With 418 platforms remaining in the North Sea, the opposition feared that sinking Brent Spar would set a dangerous precedent. Greenpeace soon became the leading source of information in what became a fierce media campaign, though it later had to apologize for having given the public false information on critical points, such as the minor importance of the poisonous remains contained in the platform. Because Shell's reaction was seen as one-sided, exaggerated and lacking insight, Greenpeace won the support of the general public. In contrast, Shell had to bear an intermittent loss in turnover of up to 30 per cent in Germany, and a similarly high percentage in other European countries.

As the developments in the Shell case demonstrate, the whole stakeholder network was dominated by an individual stakeholder, namely

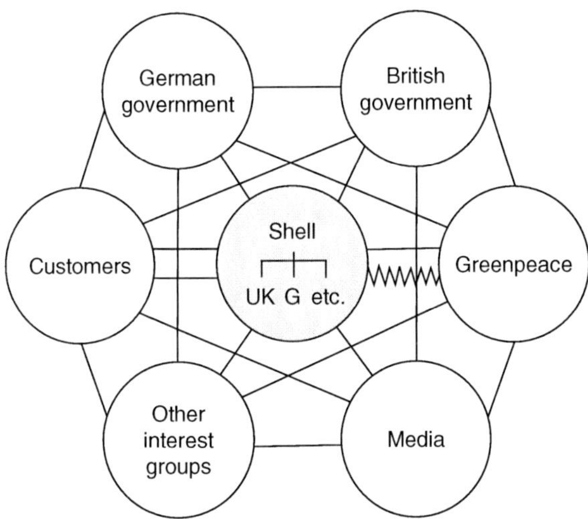


*Figure 7.1*   Shell's stakeholder network in the case example of Brent Spar: social and political stakeholders

Greenpeace. On the basis of their active roles, such stakeholders are also called the 'agents provocateurs' in a network.

## Agents provocateurs

These so-called agents provocateurs can trigger a domino effect in a network, and can thereby influence how a problem is handled by indirect mechanisms of amplification. It is of consequence for your corporation that such agents provocateurs can have significant effects, positive as well as negative, on your value-creation process via their network connections, and that the corporation often cannot or only with difficulty can exert influence on these stakeholders.

It is therefore of importance that your corporation knows the network in which it is embedded, and what kind of relationships the stakeholders in general, but also possible agents provocateurs in particular, have to each other. In the case of Brent Spar, it would have been important for Shell to have known its own position in the network in order to have built up an active relationship to its stakeholders, in this case to its customers and the German government.

This would have allowed them to have made positive use of the benefit and risk potentials of the surrounding stakeholders, and to have contained the negative effects. The German corporation Bayer provides a further example.

**Example: Bayer (German pharmaceutical and chemical corporation)**

A few years ago, it became known that suppliers of Bayer in the plant seed industry in India employ children. Mostly girls between the ages of 6 and 14 work to produce cotton seed. They work 12 hours a day and receive 50 cents for their labour. The work exposes them to dangerous pesticides which often damage their health. Since the children work all day, they cannot attend school. When the organization 'Coordination Against BAYER Hazards' (CBG) became aware of this, it began a campaign against the corporation and demanded that it end the child labour of its suppliers. As time went on, further NGOs joined the campaign, such as German World Hunger Help, German Watch, the Global March Against Child Labour and the MV Foundation. In Germany, the media focused on the situation in India and raised the question of Bayer's responsibility. Bayer partly gave in to the pressure, met with some of the NGO representatives and promised that the children would be replaced by adult labourers. Since then nothing much has happened, which is why CBG has continued its pressure and has publicly demanded that Bayer keep its promise.[2]

## Positioning

On the basis of limited awareness regarding the effect of networks, our interview partners only reported partially about isolated examples of benefit and risk potentials. This means there are potentials which could be better used in the future.

'We have an additional monitoring system, namely a media-monitoring system. We have built up a network which functions well, and also a kind of early-warning system which works internationally whenever an interesting report or development occurs somewhere. We also meet often with various people mainly from the industry. Of course they have early-warning systems too. We also have a good monitoring system regarding the dialogue with the general public. Otherwise, as I have said, when I compare it with others, then it has not been professionalized. We have no tools in this sense.'

'In Switzerland we are aware of our size. I know that I cannot afford to offend a corporation, because it might be a potential supplier or customer, a potential investor, someone influencing other customers. Individuals in these corporations are also customers, potential customers or they sit in political bodies, etc. We are aware of this network in Swiss society, and we also try to keep it in mind.'

On the basis of our experience, we see the following benefit and risk potential in positioning a corporation in a stakeholder network:

- Influence potential

In positioning yourself consciously in a network, not only are the possibilities of directly influencing stakeholder groups taken into consideration, but also those possibilities that have indirect effects via other stakeholder groups. Primarily the media but also interest groups and organizations of all kinds are the well-known influence-mediators.

'On the one hand we try to improve our work in order to offer better services for the media and on the other hand to hear from them about which issues are interesting to them and which might become interesting for us. Be it that we have to defend ourselves or prepare the defence of our viewpoints or be it that we can pick up trends and benefit from them.'

- Differentiation potential

By positioning yourself in a stakeholder network, you have the possibility of distinguishing your corporation from its competitors. Because of your corporation's position in a network, it can build up access to stakeholders having important resources in and outside the market. This way it can differentiate itself with better products and service in contrast to its main competitors, relying exclusively on direct market relationships.

> 'In this respect, we also consider the service providers. We consider the hospitals and the physiotherapists. We also take care of our network in which we work, for example with the service providers. We consider the physicians as partners with whom we cooperate and who help us to take care of complex cases.'

- Cooperation potential

On the basis of positioning in a stakeholder network, the possibilities, or at times the necessity, to cooperate with other stakeholders or segments of the stakeholder network become evident. If the cooperation can be utilized, the corporation becomes more competitive. Ignoring possibilities to cooperate may lead to difficulties, since the stakeholders could then defend their interests one-sidedly.

> 'In the interest of the stakeholders which have a long-term view, a risk-sharing model needs to be developed in which one says: 'Well, we now have an interesting medicine although we don't know how useful it is for us, but we want to investigate it. Let's study it together for five years with some ten thousand people.' Both sides share the financing and the risk. After five years at the end of the study, we have solid data. We then look at the situation anew and give the medicine a price tag. I think health insurers would have to be partners in this. I hardly see it working without the health insurers. Certainly the Federal Department of Health [Switzerland] would have to be a partner. I think that also the Federal Department of Health, which is responsible for public health, would have to bear a share. It is only possible with all the stakeholders, the financiers, the regulators and also the providers.'

## Multi-functionality

In addition, one needs to analyse the benefit-risk of a stakeholder network with multi-functional stakeholders. The multi-functional stakeholders of your corporation might be simultaneously customers, suppliers, critical citizens and shareholders. For example, the Swiss Federal authorities are such multi-functional stakeholders of Swisscom:

- Chief authority with legally binding competence for strategy guidelines.
- Regulating authority, which deregulates or regulates the telecommunications industry.
- Chief owner with a majority of the share capital.
- Large customer of many administrative departments.

In such cases the following questions are important:

- How does a multi-functional stakeholder structure its multiple-network?
- Which departments and people represent your corporation, and in what function in relation to the stakeholder? How is this coordinated?
- How do other strategically important stakeholders judge the dominance of the multi-functional stakeholder? In the case of Swisscom, are third-party shareholders attracted or repelled by the strong, multi-functional position of the Federal government, assuming that at some point it could rid itself of its share or act on the basis of its own political interests?

Therefore it is relevant for you to clarify whether there is multi-functionality in your stakeholder relations, and whether there are complementary or conflicting benefit and risk potential in the network as a result.

In our discussions with corporations, we saw that multi-functionality had not been given much attention, but that our talks quickly revealed some interesting aspects. For example, should a bank when contracting with suppliers and builders consider whether a potential contractor has an important position in its network or in that of its customers, or not? In such a case, should it turn down a better offer of a non-customer in favour of the offer of a long-term customer?

## The 'Licence to Compete'

In the market-based view, two factors determine strategic success: the attractiveness of the market structures and strategic behaviour. In order to judge the first factor of market attractiveness, there are according to Porter five major sources of influences to take into consideration. They are the competitive behaviour of the incumbent competitor, the possible market entry of new competitors, the power of the suppliers and the buyers, and the effect of substitute products. As a result of knowing about these factors, the goal is then to find a market which allows for the exploitation of a near monopolistic rent. In order for the corporation to be strategically successful with this approach, it needs to be sustainable, defensible and positioned attractively, meaning in relatively uncompetitive markets or niches. It will then have a particularly strong position in relation to its competitors and customers.[3] In any industry the stakeholders, such as customers, suppliers and regulators, are more or less competitive or cooperative depending on the relationship the corporation has built up with them. The goal of the market-based view of strategic management is that the corporation should find a relatively good competitive position in the relevant sales market. From an expanded point of view that includes both market and non-market aspects, namely the Stakeholder View, corporations systematically take into consideration the whole stakeholder network in all their undertakings. They clarify interdependencies and can broadly judge the consequences of the competitive situation for their corporation. The assessment and utilization of the possible consequences of direct and indirect relations in the stakeholder network enables the corporation to be recognized or even favoured in its competitive environment. In this way, the corporation acquires a 'Licence to Compete'.

Our discussions in this chapter allow us to conclude with the following motto:

> **A conscious position in a comprehensive stakeholder network creates strategic advantages and builds the basis for the 'Licence to Compete'.**

This perspective poses the following questions for you:

1. What does my stakeholder network look like in general or in connection to specific strategic projects?

2. Do I have an agent provocateur in my stakeholder network, and how should I deal with him or her?
3. Which benefit and risk potentials can I obtain or avoid by positioning my corporation in its stakeholder network?
4. How can I further awareness of the network of stakeholder relations in my corporation?
5. Which of my stakeholders have multiple functions, and what opportunities and risks may arise as a result of them?

## Notes

1  Locke (2002).
2  CBG (2005).
3  For example, Porter (2008, 1998, 1996, 1991; Porter and Teisberg, 2006).

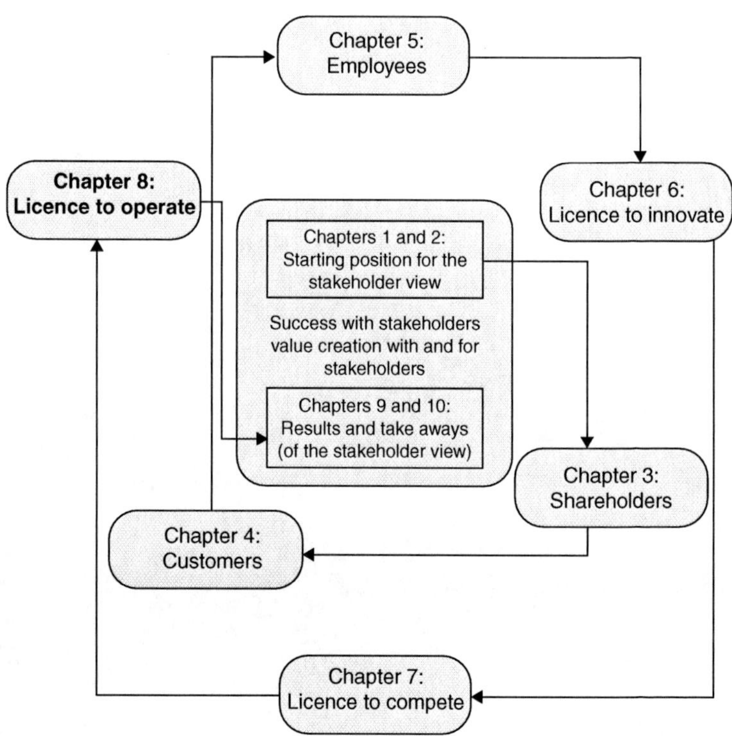

Chapter 5:
Employees

Chapter 8:
Licence to operate

Chapter 6:
Licence to innovate

Chapters 1 and 2:
Starting position for the
stakeholder view

Success with stakeholders
value creation with and for
stakeholders

Chapters 9 and 10:
Results and take aways
(of the stakeholder view)

Chapter 3:
Shareholders

Chapter 4:
Customers

Chapter 7:
Licence to compete

# 8
# The demands of society

Corporations are increasingly exposed to a critical public, which at the same time is increasingly better informed. This means that new expectations are developing in society towards your corporation as well.

## The 'Licence to Operate'

Since their conception, corporations have been embedded in a legal framework. In a sense, the legal framework is the core of their 'Licence to Operate', their authorization to do business. Today social and political groups, with their multifaceted interests and norms, are gaining increased importance. From this perspective, the 'Licence to Operate' is not just a formal instrument like the permission to operate an airline or a bank. It is the broad acceptance of business activities by the various stakeholders in society. Corporations necessarily have a prime interest in this development.

## Societal expectations

Let us approach the question with an example.

> **Example: Fisher-Price (the US toy manufacturer)**
> The speed at which the 'Licence to Operate' (here in the legal sense) can be jeopardized, and the consequences this can have, were experienced by Fisher-Price, the toy manufacturer:
> 'Toy-maker Fisher-Price is recalling 83 types of toys – including the popular Big Bird, Elmo, Dora and Diego characters – because their paint contains excessive amounts of lead ...

> The recall is the first for Fisher-Price Inc. and parent
> corporation Mattel Inc. involving lead paint … This is
> particularly alarming since Mattel, known for its strict quality
> controls, is considered a role model in the toy industry
> because of the way it operates in China.'[1]

## Laws or soft laws, that is the question

Since the case of Enron everyone is asking: 'How should a corporation
be managed so that such business scandals cannot arise?' Corporations cannot be self-service stores for greedy managers whom the
public does not condone. In this context, the question can be asked
whether corporations should take on more responsibility for themselves, subjecting themselves to codes of conduct which conform to
societal and political expectations; or whether the government, in
particular the legislative bodies, should establish order by enacting
new laws. The various political stakeholders hold differing views on
this subject. As a result of the scandals, the EU has taken the course of
a code of conduct, the so-called soft laws. National laws (in Germany,
the German Corporate Governance Code) and those for the EU (OECD
Guidelines) were developed which give corporations guidelines as to
how they can improve corporate governance.

In the USA, the Sarbanes-Oxley Act introduced new laws. This,
however, has had a negative effect on the economy. The strict regulations led to enormous administrative expenditures of time and money
for corporations. For this reason many corporations have decided to
remove themselves from the New York Stock Exchange (NYSE), such
as Swisscom,[2] Ciba,[3] E.ON,[4] Bayer[5] and BASF.[6] Also the fact that there
are fewer new listings in the New York stock market worries the NYSE.[7]

In contrast to such strict regulations, 'the creation of voluntary
frameworks has a number of advantages:

- They enable business leaders to put their values into practice
  collectively.
- They provide corporations with a measure of consistency and security in managing diverse global operations and provide quality
  controls that help deliver products that consumers want. This
  enhances trust and reputation.

- They provide benchmarks for industries, which can shame laggards into complying – or highlight breaches in standards.
- They can help share the costs of managing social and environmental risks.
- They reduce the chances of unacceptable behaviour in an industry, such as 'sweatshop' labour conditions, fraud, pollution or human rights abuses, which would damage the reputation of a sector of the global industry in general.[8]

Incidents like those at the Nestlé General Assembly in 2005 (cf. also Chapter 3) have shown that some corporations are not prepared to comply sufficiently with the expectation of important stakeholders on the basis of soft laws. Nestlé's headquarters are in Switzerland, and the Swiss Code of Best Practices of Good Corporate Governance states that a double mandate of CEO and President of the Board of Directors is possible only under special circumstances. Nestlé's Board of Directors found the provision applicable to their situation, namely that it was not possible to find a successor for the President who was leaving. Finding a successor is one of the special cases mentioned in the Code. However, the Board's arguments were not convincing, as the President was resigning on the basis of age, and this could be anticipated far enough in advance to have found a successor. Nestlé therefore had failed to adhere to the meaning of the soft laws in not taking its responsibility seriously by starting the search for a successor early enough. Instead, it entrusted the CEO with a double mandate. Many people did not find it justified to apply the exception rule in the Code of Best Practices in this case.

Such incidents, and the continuing controversy over appropriate salaries for top managers, have led various political parties to want a new law which should legally regulate these issues. In the mind of these stakeholders, the corporations missed their chance to implement voluntarily chosen principles in their particular situations in a credible way. They are apparently going to lose part of their 'Licence to Operate', because some of them chose to disregard societal and political expectations.

Our investigation of corporations has shown that today in addition to the shareholders, the customers and the employees, regulators of all kinds are regarded as essential stakeholders. This was confirmed by a discussion partner in the telecommunications sector with the following statement:

> 'Our regulator is basically friendly to competition. However, we are held back far more by legislation and politics than by the market itself. For this reason, the regulator is certainly an important stakeholder and has lost none of its importance. This will be a concern of ours for a while.'

One reason for this is the increasing number of regulations in the various industries. Many attempts to deregulate end up providing re-regulations. An illustrative example is the telecommunications industry, which was liberalized but at the same time also re-regulated. It is also of strategic relevance that corporations and industrial associations should proactively address relevant stakeholders, so as not to increase the amount of regulations by their own passivity. The Equator Principles are a good positive example.

> They were drawn up in 2003 by a group of banks working with the World Bank's International Finance Corporation (IFC). The principles are designed to ensure that financed projects are developed in a manner that is socially responsible and reflect sound environmental management practices. By the end of April 2007, they had been adopted by 51 financial institutions from 19 countries.[9]

## The corporation as global institution

In recent years, the process of globalization has accentuated the expectations of societal and political stakeholders on corporations. The corporation is one of the few global institutions capable of action in the world today. That the economy is able to globalize faster and easier than society with different political systems is not surprising. It is easier to agree globally that Coca-Cola is a fun drink than to have a unified worldwide understanding of the meaning of democracy. The cultural differences on such questions are glaring, as the USA and also the UN experienced painfully in Iraq. Samuel Huntington has already made this phenomenon an important topic of discussion with the idea of the 'Clash of Civilizations', and Robert Reich captures the essence of the conflict between 'super-capitalism' and democracy in this quote:

> Large firms became far more competitive, global, and innovative. Something I call super-capitalism was born. With this transformation, we in our capacities as consumers and investors have done significantly better. In our capacities as citizens seeking the common good, however, we have lost ground.[10]

Corporations with turnovers greater than the gross domestic product of a small country demonstrate (compare Figure 8.1 below) that not only are they globally active, but also they can be extremely successful in doing so. Examples like Nestlé, Pfizer, Shell, Marks & Spencer, etc. confirm this explicitly. It is precisely because of their global ability to achieve results and recognition that the expectations

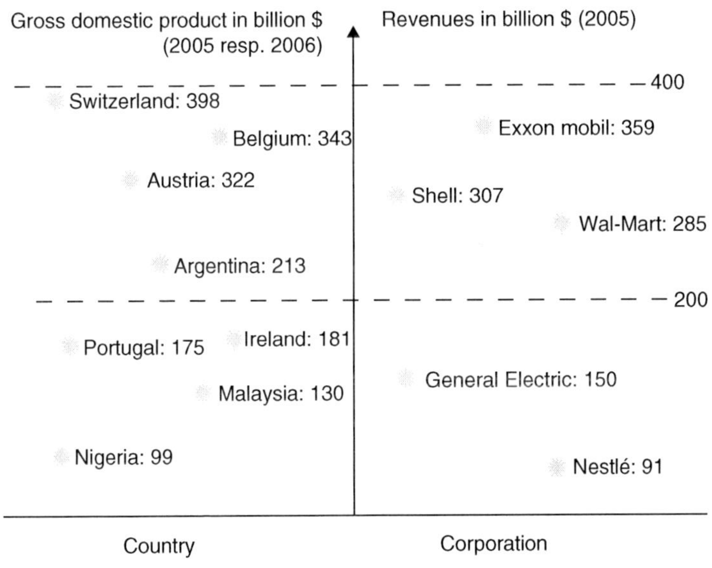


*Figure 8.1* Comparison of gross domestic product and the total revenue of corporations

*Sources*: The gross national product of countries can be seen on the homepage of the US Department of State: http://www.state.gov/r/pa/ei/bgn/. Since not all countries had figures for the year 2006, some figures for 2005 were used. The total revenue figures were taken from the respective annual reports.

of not only their economic role but also their role in society have become relevant.

Particularly difficult questions may arise when a corporation does business in a region that is politically and ecologically sensitive. In 1995, for example, shortly after the already-mentioned Brent Spar incident, Shell was confronted with the added claim that, as a global player in a country like Nigeria, it had to assume ecological and political responsibility. Let us look more closely at this case, which is exemplary in demonstrating the problematic aspects of the societal responsibility of a corporation.

**Example: Shell (Dutch-British oil and gas concern)**
Shell Petroleum Development Corporation of Nigeria (SPDC) has been producing oil in Nigeria since 1958. In 1995 it was the leading player in a joint-venture consisting of the Nigerian National Petroleum Corporation (55 per cent), Shell (30 per cent), Elf (10 per cent) and Agip (5 per cent). This joint-venture produced almost a million barrels of oil per day, which was about half of the total Nigerian production, which was 3 per cent of world production. (In 2004 Nigeria produced 2.5 million barrels of oil daily, which corresponded to about 3 per cent of the worldwide demand; about 1 million barrels of oil were produced by Shell and its joint-venture partners.) The production of oil was Nigeria's most important industry, responsible for 90 per cent of the export trade and 80 per cent of the national income (in 2002 oil and gas made up 98 per cent of the export income and about 83 per cent of the national income). For these reasons, the production of oil played and still plays an important role in Nigeria's economic and social development.

Aside from its economic contribution, Shell spent US$20 million for social development programmes, such as building schools, hospitals, waterworks and agricultural development. Despite this engagement, Shell was held responsible by environmental and human rights organizations for the heavy pollution and exploitation of the environment in the Niger Delta, and especially in the river states where the Ogoni live.

The Ogoni are an ethnic group of about 500,000 people who live on 460 square miles of the Niger Delta. In 1990 they founded the 'Movement for the Survival of Ogoni People' (MOSOP), which fought for greater political autonomy, for a larger portion of the oil income as compensation for environmental damage and against the financial discrimination of the region. Although there are enormous oil reserves in the region, the Ogoni are extremely poor. In 1995 the gross social product per person lay below the national average of US$280, though efforts had been made to distribute the resources so as to favour a larger portion of the poor population. After the Ogoni had expressed their demands to the government, between 1991 and 1993 they changed their tactics and addressed Shell directly. Their main goal was to make their situation known in Europe and the USA, hoping that people there would be more open and sympathetic to their problems than their own government were.

In connection with clashes between the two Ogoni parties, in which four opinion leaders lost their lives, Ken Saro Wiwa, the leader of the radical wing of the protest movement, and eight further members of the party were accused of criminal acts against the Nigerian government. In spite of international protest, they were found guilty of inciting riots and thereby causing the deaths of the four Ogoni leaders. They were executed by the military junta of General Sani Abacha.

In the course of these events, public opinion around the world held Shell accountable. In addition to being responsible for polluting the environment, exploiting the natural resources, burning petrol stations, operating antiquated equipment, supporting a brutal regime and hence indirectly the repression of the Ogoni, and failing to compensate the landowners, Shell was especially blamed for failing to support sufficiently the interests of the Ogoni with the Nigerian government, and for not attempting to have Ken Saro Wiwa and the other eight members pardoned.

Internationally politicians and organizations like Greenpeace reacted by calling for a boycott of Nigeria and Shell, in order that Shell stop its activities in Nigeria.

Shell rejected all the accusations, saying that its policy of neutrality regarding internal affairs required restraint in the conflict between the Nigerian government and the Ogoni.

> Shell also rejected any political responsibility, while at the
> same time accepting its responsibility for the environment.
> Shell underlined the fact that part of the environmental
> problems were due to sabotage and the agricultural practices of
> the people. Old equipment in poor condition would be
> replaced piece by piece. Regarding the scant compensation of
> the Ogoni, Shell was successful in influencing the government,
> and acknowledged its own obligation to create greater welfare
> among the people. In spite of these efforts, the situation in
> Nigeria remains very complex and so far no simple solutions
> have been possible.

What is certain is that global corporations, like Shell in this case, can hardly keep themselves from becoming involved in political situations and responsibilities. Particularly in this regard, paying professional attention to stakeholder relations is indispensable. For a corporation doing business internationally, it is an indispensable part of the duties of management.

## Interest groups

Interest groups are often non-profit organizations. They are not primarily oriented towards business, but rather follow a purpose, which places the promotion or support of its members, or the pursuit of an idealistic concern, in the foreground. Among them in the recent past are also many known non-governmental organizations (NGOs), such as Amnesty International and Greenpeace. In practically all industrial countries, these interest groups are gaining importance, as Figure 8.2 illustrates. Also the comments of one of our interviewees in the financial service sector confirms this:

> 'I see the potential for change primarily with the unconventional
> stakeholders, to which the NGOs clearly belong. There is a lot of
> movement there. This area is becoming more and more important
> for us.'

Such organizations often come about in order to fill a gap between the market economy and the state in making certain goods and services available. For example, social integration or political, cultural and charitable activities are often accomplished better by such organizations than by the public or market institutions. NGOs are

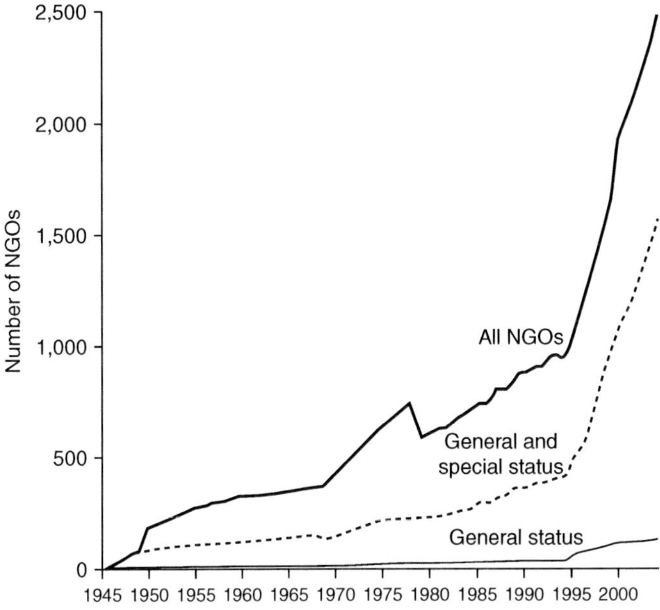


*Figure 8.2*   The growing number of NGOs with ECOSOC consultative status
(Economic and Social Council of the US)
*Source*: Based on Willetts (2004).

therefore economic, societal or political mediators in the area of
tension between the market and the state.

In this connection, your corporation could find out whether its own
relevant interest groups are those that function primarily as warning
systems or those that seek to solve problems together with the corporation. This is decisive for determining which behavioural pattern to
aim for in order to be able to use a stakeholder group as a resource.
The method of analysis presented in Chapter 2 is applicable here.

The following example shows that fruitful cooperation through
dialogue with stakeholder interest groups is possible.

> **Example: Starbucks (US coffee purveyor)**
> Since 2000 Starbucks has worked together with TransFair, a US
> organization, that seeks to ensure that producers receive a fair
> price for their products, whether they be coffee, tea, bananas,

> mangoes, sugar or rice. By working together, Starbucks has
> agreed 'to sourcing, roasting and selling Fair Trade Certified
> coffee through its network'. Since the beginning of this joint
> venture, the amount of Fair Trade coffee that Starbucks has
> bought has doubled. Starbucks is also working in other areas
> with TransFair, such as marketing, product development, and
> building up industry connections.[11]

Robert Reich writes on the topic of working with stakeholders:

> Some believe corporate boards should represent all 'stakeholders' –
> including employees, communities, and society in general – and
> view this notion of corporate governance as the answer for how
> to reconcile the interests of investors with those of the rest of
> society. The idea of 'stakeholder capitalism' was, you recall, put for-
> ward by Walter Lippmann, Adolf Berle, and Gardiner Means in the
> early twentieth century, and it found expression in the 'corporate
> statesmen' of the Not Quite Golden Age.[12]

## Stakeholder democracy

A corporation is clearly required not only by the market but also
forces outside the market to act within a stakeholder network (also
see Chapter 7). What is important in doing so is not just the ability to be competitive, but mainly to be credible. The corporation's
purpose and its business practices need to be acceptable to the society as a whole. With two consecutive wake-up calls (Brent Spar and
Nigeria), Shell had to learn that it was not enough to produce and
sell a good product, but that a corporation and its behaviour also
have to be acceptable to society. In the telecommunications industry,
corporations had to learn to take the expectations of society into consideration in building their networks and necessary antennae. Society
is a difficult phenomenon to grasp if one does not see it as a network
of non-market stakeholders, all attempting to bring their interest to
bear in a more or less democratic process. Such a network is extremely
difficult to manage and quickly exceeds the possibilities of an individual corporation. For this reason, a corporation needs to understand
that it should gain and maintain access to the appropriate network in
order to be an actor in it. It is not primarily about a 'Licence to Compete' in the usual market sense (compare Chapter 7), but rather that

your corporation should cultivate its relationships to other stakeholders in order to thereby create the basis of credibility and acceptance for your business activities.

Especially in political situations which are not part of daily business, it is important to be able to listen and then to respond appropriately to the concerns of the non-market surroundings. On the basis of the painful experience in Nigeria, Shell developed the principle of 'listening and responding' in order to maintain its societal 'Licence to Operate'. In so doing, the corporation achieved a higher level of corporate professionalism, which is absolutely necessary today for any corporation acting globally in a critical industry. Telecommunications corporations have also professionalized their dialogue with the societal stakeholders.

The motto of 'listening and responding', however, requires a healthy critical attitude on the part of management regarding the concerns of the various interest groups. Not all of their concerns are always and exclusively in the interest of the groups or the ideas for which they consider themselves to be the advocates. For example, shortly before the Brent Spar campaign Greenpeace had noticed a reduction in its membership. The interest of Greenpeace in the Brent Spar campaign served not only ecological motives, but also its own economic ones. Similar situations can also occur with other interest groups or with the media when under competitive pressure. Management has to wrestle with these issues, and to consider them when 'responding'.

Corporations which want to integrate the political relevance or societal consequences of their activities into their strategic management often create a Department of Public Affairs within their organization. Our interview partners in both industries emphasized this repeatedly:

'For politics and the regulators, there are specially created areas in the organization. There are special positions that concern themselves with the stakeholders. They have the legal skills and also the special competence for contact and discussions with the regulators for example.'

'The Group Public Affairs (GPA) improved the monitoring of the political domain considerably. With GPA the observation of the ongoing legislative proceedings could be systematized and improved. Activities in the area of public affairs (lobbying) were

initiated in a more goal-directed and successful manner than they had been previously.'

All this does not exclude the fact that outstanding managers also have to face the public personally. Here is the opinion of a self-assured interview partner:

'What do I do regarding the public? I assume the role I have to, by which I mean I represent the corporation. For this reason I am present in the media, and also why I either defend or explain decisions which in part I had no responsibility in making. I take on the responsibility, which means I represent the corporation.'

Our discussion in this chapter can conclude with the following motto:

**Credibility and professionalism in relation to society and political issues are an indispensable basis for a corporation to receive its 'Licence to Operate'.**

For your corporation the following questions could be relevant:

1. What societal expectation could confront my corporation on a local or global level?
2. Which societal and political stakeholders are relevant on the basis of my strategic issues?
3. To what extent do the values of my strategically relevant societal and political stakeholders differ from those of my corporation?
4. How is my corporation represented externally on matters of societal concern?
5. To what extent does my corporation have to observe corporate specific or industry specific or generally valid soft laws in order to avoid risks and make use of opportunities?

## Notes

1  CNN (2007).
2  Swisscom (2007).
3  NZZ (2007).
4  Reuters (2007).
5  Forbes (2007).
6  BASF (2007).
7  BBC (2006a); BBC (2006b).
8  Tomorrow's Company (2007), p. 22.
9  Tomorrow's Company (2007), p. 23.
10  Reich (2007), p. 7.
11  Starbucks (2005).
12  Reich (2007), pp. 176–7.

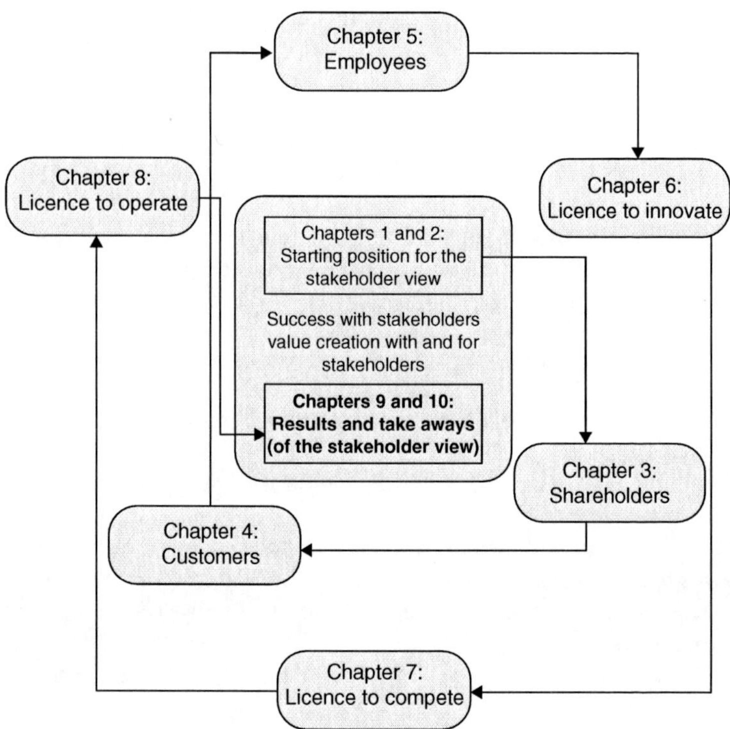

Chapter 5:
Employees
Chapter 8:
Licence to operate
Chapter 6:
Licence to innovate
Chapters 1 and 2:
Starting position for the
stakeholder view
Success with stakeholders
value creation with and for
stakeholders
Chapters 9 and 10:
Results and take aways
(of the stakeholder view)
Chapter 3:
Shareholders
Chapter 4:
Customers
Chapter 7:
Licence to compete

# 9
# Transparency and sustainability

Now the question arises of how to communicate with one's stakeholders. The following anecdote of Paul Watzlawick[1] illustrates how not to:

A man wants to hang up a picture. He has a nail but no hammer. He realizes that his neighbour probably has a hammer he could borrow. But then he remembers that yesterday the neighbour had not been particularly friendly when they met. Perhaps he would be unwilling to lend his hammer. So the man carries on this conversation with himself, asking questions and answering them the way he imagines the neighbour might. All of this is coloured by his own negative thinking. In the end, he is so infuriated by his spiteful assumptions that he storms over to the neighbour's and bangs on his door like a crazy man. When the neighbour opens it, he screams at him, 'Then in that case, keep your stupid hammer.' It goes without saying that the neighbour has no way of knowing what is going on or what caused the outburst.

While we hope that the dialogue with your stakeholders will not be like this, we know that problems can arise, especially with stakeholders whom we do not know well. In such cases, it is advisable to prevent prejudice and misunderstanding from arising from the start. The important thing is the way that corporate activities are made transparent to the stakeholders. A positive example can be noted in the following:

The Extractive Industries Transparency Initiative (EITI), launched in June 2003, aims to increase transparency in transactions between governments and corporations within extractive industries. Participants include government, industry, and civil society representatives.[2]

From this point of view, comprehensive sustainability reporting is indispensable today on the corporate level. Thus far, however, the annual reports of corporations have been primarily financial reports. The demand for information on societal and ecological activity, and in particular on sustainability, is increasing rapidly; also in the public domain, as an example in Germany shows:

> In the future, Germany's state controlled enterprises will need to fulfil the same criteria of transparency as corporations on the stock market. This year (2007) the Federal Cabinet is supposed to decide on introducing a 'Public Corporate Governance Code'.[3]

Two tendencies can be seen in the reporting system for corporations:

1. Corporations with business activities that affect society as well as the environment are providing additional detailed reports on questions pertaining to these areas;
2. More and more corporations are developing integrated reporting systems with business, societal and ecological elements. Examples of this are Novo Nordisk, German Telecom, Henkel and Roche, with a strong upward trend. The level of integration, however, differs significantly in practice. Most often the more obvious topics are dealt with, such as human resource management, health care and safety, or product safety. Basic questions, such as those pertaining to sustainability, are rarely worked into the reports.

KPMG writes in this regard:

> The think-tank SustainAbility reports that although around two-thirds (70%) of corporations report some interaction with investors on sustainability matters, many reports still lack the hard targets and forward-looking information that makes for required reading for analysts. It expects to see a progressive hardening of information requirements regarding sustainability; a steady shift towards non-OECD country issues and perspectives; and a growing focus on value creation, business models and scalable entrepreneurial solutions to sustainability challenges.[4]

Your corporation needs to ask itself how it wants to manage its reporting.

## Sustainability

Challenged by occurrences already mentioned in the previous chapters, progressive corporations have developed concepts for comprehensive sustainability and have made noticeable progress in implementing them. 'Sustainable development is described as development which satisfies the needs of the generation of today without endangering the chances of future generations to satisfy their needs.' This definition was formulated in 1987 by a UN Commission under the leadership of the former Norwegian Prime Minister Gro Harlem Brundtland. This perspective, which includes social and natural factors in addition to economic ones, has actually become the focus of a growing number of enterprises. Here are two quotes from the corporations studied, showing that they are already striving for a comprehensive perspective in this regard:

> 'Economically, ecologically and socially intelligent long-term activities are what we call 'sustainable corporate management.' Sustainable corporate management is in the interest of all stakeholders, because in the final analysis it benefits everyone the most. It can therefore be considered the condition for a corporation's long-term success.'

> 'The task of sustainable management is making instruments and indicators available, and making a contribution to the bottom line and general success. In this respect we have not fulfilled the task yet. We also haven't defined precisely what the relevant aspects and what the core indicators are, in human resource management for example.'

A majority of the cases shows that 'sustainability' can still be interpreted very differently, as one interviewee emphasizes:

> 'The word sustainability in my opinion is still largely misused. For me, sustainability clearly includes the following three aspects: economic success, social responsibility and environmental responsibility. In this respect, I would say that we are comparatively

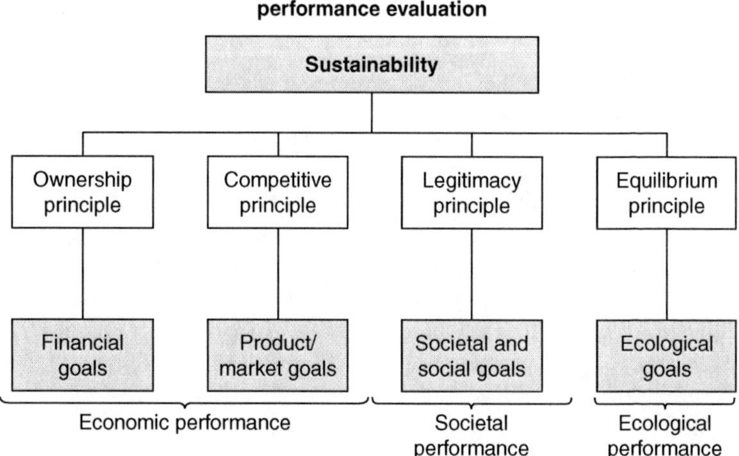


*Figure 9.1* Sustainability, goal-setting principles and performance assessment

sustainable... I believe it is already part of our culture to use common sense in order to estimate what is in fact sustainable. What is possible in this corporation? What is also going to be profitable in the long run?'

Looked at comprehensively, sustainability leads a corporation to consider a number of principles in the process of formulating its goals, and that in the end there has to be evidence not only of economic but also of societal and ecological performance, as shown in Figure 9.1.

## General principles of corporations

The consideration of four fundamental principles can help your corporation become sustainable in an economic, societal and ecological direction:

1. Property rights enable the acquisition, ownership, use and consumption of material as needed by a corporation. The principle of

property rights also allows the ownership of a corporation to seek to increase its property. In a traditional sense in a joint-stock corporation, this principle often leads to being oriented to financial demands, i.e. shareholder value (compare Chapter 3). In a market economy, financial success is an existential condition for a corporation, and therefore part of the Licence to Operate (compare Chapter 8);

2. Customer needs are primary from the standpoint of the principle of competition. In a competitive situation, corporations are continually challenged to come up with innovations, and to distinguish themselves from the competition with their economic achievements which are their products and services, in order to gain more customers. From this perspective, the 'Licence to Compete' (compare Chapter 7) and the 'Licence to Innovate' (compare Chapter 6) are of central importance;

3. As already mentioned, every corporation is also a societal institution. Therefore societal goals are relevant. Social goals concerning employees attempt to understand and consider the needs and demands of the employees. To obtain the 'Licence to Operate' (compare Chapter 8), a legitimizing principle always underlies the articulation of business goals;

4. The consideration of the natural environment in formulating business goals can be understood by the principle of equilibrium. From this perspective, the corporation must seek an equilibrium with the natural environment in respect to its goals. The examination of these considerations contributes to the 'Licence to Operate' (see Chapter 8).

## Matching goals and principles

If you take into consideration all four principles (principle of property rights, principle of competition, principle of legitimacy, and principle of equilibrium) in formulating goals, then there are four categories of business goals for a corporation: namely financial goals, product/market goals, societal goals and ecological goals.

Financial goals can be deduced from the financial value creation and revenue process. In the foreground are the goals of providing the corporation with sufficient capital and maintaining liquidity, in addition to giving appropriate consideration and compensation to those bearing the financial risks. An optimal capital and asset structure takes financial as well as corporate risks into account. Important stakeholders for reporting from this point of view are the shareholders, the lenders, the investors in general and the financial analysts.

The product/market performance goals refer to the value creation and revenue processes. Therefore they have to do with the organization of the business processes, necessary for ensuring a sustainable and defensible competitive situation. Foremost are the market and product goals which the corporation has set itself to meet. Then there are the research and development goals, and the goals concerning the acquisition and application of resources. Primarily, the customers, the suppliers and the external know-how partners need to be provided with reporting on pertinent information in the categories of goals.

As explained before, every corporation is also a societal institution, and therefore societal goals are relevant. Social goals regarding employees attempt to understand and to consider the needs and demands of the employees. For example, such goals can include fair wages, profit sharing, good working conditions, equal opportunity and social benefits. In accordance with the many goal possibilities, there are also many ways of providing employees with information.

The corporation's societal goals are also oriented to the expectations of its relevant societal stakeholders, such as local authorities; its reporting is oriented accordingly.

The corporation is always embedded in an ecological system whose equilibrium it influences. A consequence of this is to have ecological goals. The corporation uses and processes natural resources in various ways. As a rule its input is resources of limited supply, while in addition to the actual market performance (products and services), its output is a variety of emissions and waste (i.e. liquid waste, exhaust fumes, noise), which are passed on to the environment. In addition, corporation activities often necessarily bring potential health and environmental hazards with them, which manifest themselves over time in repeated accidents or damage of various kinds. The relevant target groups for ecological reporting are primarily the advocates of the ecosystems, which are often organized as NGOs, as well as the general public.

In measuring performance, the goal categories discussed above are often referred to together as the triple bottom line.

## Triple bottom line

The triple bottom line is an extension of the financial bottom line, and thereby the performance certificate of the comprehensive and sustainable performance of a corporation.

Regarding the economic performance aside from the interests of the investors, there are also the sustainable needs and expectations of other market stakeholders, such as customers and suppliers. An interview partner in the area of telecommunications sees it this way:

'It is actually completely clear. There is a main indicator in our business and that is the EBITDA (Earnings Before Interest, Taxes, Depreciation and Amortization), in the end it is all about the net profit. And then, depending on the area you work in but often only in limited areas, it is the turn-over, then more the investments, the responsible attitude regarding the investment budget or customer satisfaction, etc. Externally we mostly use the so-called ARPU (average revenue per user).'

Generally the performance indicators mentioned in the paragraphs on product/market goals are in the foreground. The purely financial performance indicators (Return on investment (ROI), cash flow, etc.) are not discussed any further here.

Regarding the product/market performance of a corporation, the main consideration is ensuring quality of life for people, including the employees, today and also in the future by providing valuable products and services, and supportive conditions. Health can be given as an example. Corporations are investing increasingly in preventive measures, in that they offer their employees exercise programmes or continuing education programmes for sensible nutrition and promoting health. This is also an expression of sustainable and comprehensive performance thinking in the sense of the societal and social goals mentioned above.

Awareness of social performance in individual corporations is confirmed by the following statement:

'For social performance, I think the indicators are primarily the general sum of our activities as employers, how we act as employers monetarily and non-monetarily.'

The greatest progress in the last 20 years has no doubt been achieved in ecological performance, meaning in the consideration of naturally given factors and limitations.

> 'This is being practised. We are already doing that. The environment team responsible for it really cares about its stakeholders, and in terms of its role also does justice to its responsibility for the environment.'

> 'We are certified according to ISO 14001, and one of the demands is to improve continually the environmentally relevant aspects.'

A number of corporations worldwide have introduced ecological standards, according to which their ecological goals in the production and distribution of their products and services are inspected:

> The ISO 14064 standards for greenhouse gas accounting and verification published on 1 March 2006 resulted from the work of some 175 international experts from 45 countries, and 11 international business, development or environmental organizations.[5]

This often leads, on the one hand, to an improvement of corporation procedures regarding emissions and to a more economical use of natural resources. On the other hand, it has also often led to more innovative products and services. In the end in many cases, both had a positive influence on the financial success of these corporations because, for example by preventing environmental damage, the incurring costs could be avoided.

The Nobel Peace Prize for Al Gore and the IPCC (Intergovernmental Panel on Climate Change) for their efforts on behalf of climate change has caused this topic to become more important. All over the world, corporations are trying to develop industry standards in order to stop climate change. These developments are also becoming increasingly relevant for your corporation.

## Measure it all

Sustainability can certainly be regarded as a success formula for your corporation. Sometimes scepticism occurs where sustainable measures have been introduced, if their success is not immediately monetarily measurable. Corporations are primarily subject to the pressure of quantification by investors and financial analysts. We are familiar with the problems of quantification in politics as well. As long as there was no clearly measurable proof that our civilization is affecting climate change, it was difficult to find enough countries willing to take preventive action. Measurability, however, must not be the sole criterion for our decisions. There are relationships which are important, even if they cannot be quantified. To quote Einstein: 'Not every thing that counts is countable, and not every thing that can be counted, counts!'

The measurability of sustainable performance is made particularly difficult by the long-term perspective involved, which brings with it a high degree of uncertainty, as do the dynamic and network influences of strategically relevant stakeholders. In this regard, there are indeed parallels to certain economic performance measurements. In the financial appraisal of corporations, for example, as a rule a number of assumptions are made to eliminate the existing uncertainties and to simplify the calculating process. However, these assumptions are often not mentioned when considering the results. For example, customer needs are changing at an ever-increasing pace in many industries, and are being largely influenced by different stakeholders such as consumer organizations, NGOs and regulators.

For the individual performance categories, but also for all three of the summarized dimensions in the triple bottom line, various indicator-sets have been developed in practice and in the literature. So far the indicator problem has been most difficult to apply in the area of society. This is not surprising as it is here that the above-mentioned quantification difficulties arise. For this reason, societal performance is often evaluated with qualitative indicators and process procedures.

Table 9.1 shows examples of indicators that are already in use today. You can choose an indicator-set which best corresponds to the stakeholder situation in your corporation (i.e. ISO 14001 for ecologically vulnerable operations), and complement it individually.

## Social performance pays off

As already mentioned, the measurement and consideration of societal performance provide the greatest difficulties. In the discussion, of

*Table 9.1*  Economic, social and ecological indicators

| Indicator | Homepage address |
| --- | --- |
| **Economic performance** | |
| Traditional indicators (especially shareholder value) | |
| IAS (International Accounting Standard) | http://www.iasb.org.uk |
| ISO 9000 | http://www.iso.ch |
| EFQM (European Foundation for Quality Management) | http://www.efqm.org |
| **Social and societal performance** | |
| SA Social Accountability 8000 | http://www.sa-intl.org/ |
| AA Account Ability 1000 | http://www.accountability.org.uk |
| Global Compact | http://www.unglobalcompact.org |
| Global Sullivan Principles | http://www.thesullivanfoundation.org/gsp/default.asp |
| **Ecological performance** | |
| ISO 14001 | http://www.iso.ch |
| Earth Summit (extended to social / societal areas) | http://www.earthsummit2002.org |
| EMAS (Eco-Management and Audit Scheme) | http://www.emas.org.uk |
| **Economic, societal and ecological performance** | |
| TBL (Triple Bottom Line ) GRI (Global Reporting Initiative) | http://www.globalreporting.org |
| Balanced Scorecard | http://www.balancescorecard.org |
| WMS (Value Management System) | http://www.dnwe.de/2/content/bb_01.htm |
| Life Cycle Assessment | http://www.uneptie.org/en/about/index.htm |
| ISO 26000 | http://isotc.iso.org/livelink/livelink/fetch/2000/2122/830949/3934883/3935096/home.html?nodeid=4451259&vernum=0 |

whether it makes any sense to consider societal criteria in the area of
business performance, there are two opposing theses:

1. *Harmony thesis*: The consideration of the demands of societal
   stakeholder promotes the legitimatization and acceptance of the
   corporation by the society and contributes to the security of its
   long-term existence. There are also parallel factors, for example the
   satisfaction of the employees promotes their motivation as well as
   corporation success.

2. *Antinomy thesis*: Stakeholder demands and their consideration are illegitimate, because they lead to a suboptimal use of resources; the corporation's efficiency is thereby weakened. The contrast between economic and societal efficiency is evident here.

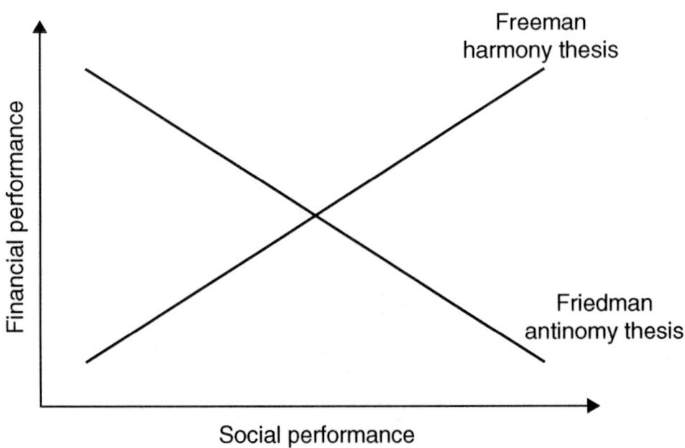


*Figure 9.2*   Relationship between financial and social success
*Notes*: Social Performance: Consideration for example fulfilling the demands of a broad circle of stakeholders. Financial Performance: Consideration for example fulfilling the demands of shareholders/owners.
*Source*: Based on Preston and O'Bannon (1997).

These two theses, presented schematically in Figure 9.2, are represented approximately by R. Edward Freeman (harmony thesis) and by Milton Friedman (antinomy thesis).

Often cost considerations are brought up in this context: if one considers the stakeholder demands from the point of view of their immediate effect on cost, then one can say that they may lead to a rise in costs, because of possible negotiating expenses as well as resource contribution to stakeholders. On the other hand, the consideration of stakeholder issues may reduce costs, since the risk potential as well as higher PR and legitimization expenses and perhaps even legal costs can be reduced. There are additional indirect effects, such as cost savings due to using stakeholder knowledge for value creation.

For you, the question is which of the two effects is greater in the case of your corporation. In this regard, the evidence and empirical studies are growing. In over 100 scientific studies, the harmony thesis was confirmed empirically. According to these studies, good financial performance is the primary basis for good societal performance. An investigation by Morgan Stanley and Oekom Research found that sustainable corporations in the years 1999–2003 had a 23 per cent better stock market rate than their competition.[6]

*Table 9.2*   Sustainable criteria industry analysis

| Topic areas | Criteria examples |
| --- | --- |
| Business policy | Quality of the sustainability reporting, corporate governance |
| Management | Organization and responsibility for sustainability, environmental management |
| Business/production | Key figures on $CO_2$ emissions, energy/water use, waste management |
| Products | Life cycle analyses, environment and social label |
| Employees | Work-life-balance, employee satisfaction, education and continuing education |
| Stakeholders | Active stakeholder dialogue, environmental and social standards for suppliers |

*Source:* ZKB (2007).

## Value transparency

The already mentioned triple bottom line is an instrument with which a corporation's performance record can be shown in the three areas of economics, society and ecology. The evaluation is heading in the right direction, but includes only selected aspects. It would be especially desirable to be able to establish the added value creation contributed by all the stakeholders. The evaluation would need to provide information about which benefit potentials certain stakeholder-oriented measures increase, and which risk potentials they reduce.

Lacking an accepted measurement for stakeholder value, corporations use helpful quantifiers, as the following example shows:

> **Example: pharmaceutical corporations**
> Pharmaceutical corporations are experiencing a slump at the moment regarding their ability to innovate. Although they continue to place new products on the market, these are mostly follow-ups which provide only a relatively minor improvement over their prototypes. This has led to mistrust on the part of health insurers, which see in the new products increasing costs (and hence increases in the premiums of policy holders) rather than any real innovation. In order to

rebuild trust but also to generally improve collaboration with the health insurers, it is important for the pharmaceutical corporations to intensify their relationship to this stakeholder. In a concrete case, the following indicators were used as basic data for building trust and as indicators for increasing the appropriate stakeholder values:

- Increasing number of contacts with the health care companies;
- Number of follow-up meetings;
- Rank in the publications of health insurers (e.g. member newsletters);
- Number of articles written jointly.

Of importance is finding indicators for stakeholder value which can be accepted by all the partners involved, and which are significant for judging the value creation of certain actions in the eyes of the corporation as well as the stakeholders.

The indicators and variables mentioned need to be used for not only external reporting, but also important quality control within the corporation. They can be the basis for MbO (Management by Objectives), as well as for overseeing the implementation of a stakeholder-oriented strategy. An example of this can be found at Shell.

**Example: Shell**
Corporation guidelines often have little effect unless there is a rigorous method of implementing them. At the time we analysed the corporation, the managers of all Shell enterprises worldwide were obliged to write and sign three separate letters annually about performance in the following areas: business integrity, health, safety and environment, as well as propagating and explaining the general business principles to the employees. These letters were confirmation for the directors of the group holding corporations that the relevant guidelines had been accepted, the methods were being implemented, and that their adherence was guaranteed.

Our presentation in this chapter can be concluded with the following motto:

**The extension of shareholder value to a comprehensive stakeholder value based on indicators makes a corporation more transparent, and can verify sustainable success in a more differentiated manner.**

The following questions may be relevant for your corporation:

1. What is the meaning of sustainability in my corporation? Does it include all four basic principles (property rights, competition, legitimization and equilibrium)?
2. How is my conception of sustainability reflected in my goals?
3. Which indicators or instruments do I use, in order to encourage the sustainability of my value creation process, and also to make the process transparent to my strategically relevant stakeholders?

## Notes

1  Watzlawick (1988).
2  Tomorrow's-Company (2007), p. 23.
3  CASHdaily (2007b), p. 6.
4  Tomorrow's-Company (2007), p. 15.
5  Tomorrow's-Company (2007), p. 23
6  Oekom Research (2003).

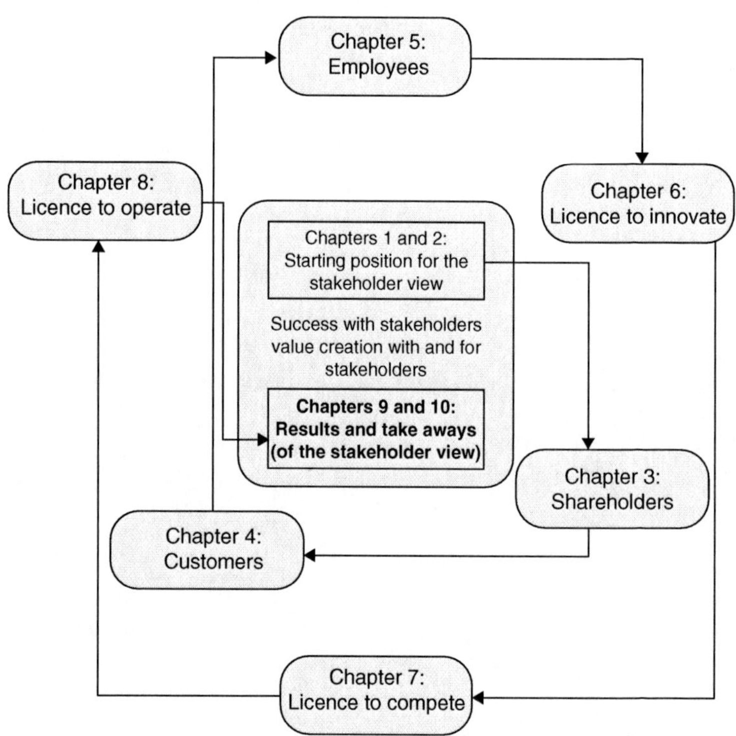

Chapter 5:
Employees
Chapter 8:
Licence to operate
Chapter 6:
Licence to innovate
Chapters 1 and 2:
Starting position for the
stakeholder view
Success with stakeholders
value creation with and for
stakeholders
Chapters 9 and 10:
Results and take aways
(of the stakeholder view)
Chapter 3:
Shareholders
Chapter 4:
Customers
Chapter 7:
Licence to compete

# 10
# Have your cake and eat it

In the last chapters, we have shown how you can increase the success of your corporation as a whole by consciously paying attention to stakeholder relationships. In the long run, this is only possible by treating your stakeholders fairly. By this we mean that the stakeholders should be able to expect something in return for their engagement with the corporation. This is not compatible with giving preferential treatment to one stakeholder category, e.g. the top managers.

When Percy Barnevik, who for years had been idolized and highly paid as Mr ABB, resigned, he had himself paid an additional 148 million Swiss francs as a retirement benefit. When this became public, he justified himself by saying that he needed this amount to maintain the standard of living to which he was accustomed. How does this make a normal ABB retiree feel, after years of assisting implementation of Mr Barnevik's corporate strategies, when he only receives a pension of a few thousand francs a month? Alarmed by the public outcry regarding Barnevik's excess, ABB attempted to contain the damage by asking for some of the money back. After some years of negotiating, Barnevik and ABB agreed that the former CEO would pay back 90 million francs. As a result, only 58 million francs remained as his retirement benefit.[1]

Another example is the CEO of Merrill Lynch:

Stan O'Neal, the former head of the US investment bank Merrill Lynch, receives a severance payment of 161.5 million US dollars. [He] has had to resign, because the bank ended the third quarter with a loss of 2.3 billion dollars. This was due to failed investments in the area of mortgage and credit. On the same day, a lawsuit was brought against the bank. The financial institution is accused of having violated stock market regulations. Among the accused is former Chief Executive O'Neal. In the last five years he earned 60 million dollars. The resignation was declared 'retirement'. This way he is able to keep the entire severance payment.[2]

What is required is a fair system of disseminating value, in order that stakeholders are prepared to engage themselves positively in the value-creation process. Incentives need to be created so that stakeholders will make firm-specific investments. A glance at the practice today shows that more and more corporations are thinking about what their corporate responsibility is in this regard. In addition to complete reporting, which we addressed in the previous chapter, increasingly positions such as Ethical Officer, Diversity Manager or advisors to the board of directors are being created. At Roche, Nestlé and Credit Suisse, committees have been created within the executive boards which concern themselves with sustainability and Corporate Social Responsibility.

## The upside-down pyramid

The term 'Corporate Social Responsibility' (CSR) arose in the 1950s. Mainly the idea stood for extending a narrowly understood economic responsibility of a corporation to include social responsibility. Due to the fact that corporations have a great deal of social influence, the sole focus on the financial aspect was increasingly criticized. The main question today in a comprehensive sense is to whom and for what a corporation is responsible. A well-known concept of comprehensive corporate responsibility is represented in the graph in Figure 10.1 below.

In the first tier of the responsibility pyramid, the purely economic responsibility of the corporation dominates according to the classic economic ideas of Adam Smith, in which the often-cited 'invisible hand' of the market automatically transforms self-interest into the common good. It is the responsibility of the corporation to face the challenges of the market. The importance of this responsibility is underlined by Nobel Prize winner Milton Friedman:

In such an economy [a free economy], there is one and only one social responsibility of business – to use its resources and engage in

*Figure 10.1*   Concept of comprehensive corporate responsibility
*Source*: Carroll (1991), p. 42. Reprinted from *Business Horizons*, Vol. 34, No. 1991, Carroll, A. B. 'The Pyramid of Corporate Social Responsibility: Toward the Moral Management of Organizational Stakeholders', pp. 39–48, 1991, with permission from Elsevier.

activities designed to increase its profits so long as it stays within the rules of the game, which is to say, engages in open and free competition, without deception or fraud.[3]

Thereby Friedman concluded in his book *Capitalism and Freedom* that corporations are responsible only for making the most profit possible for their shareholders. However, today there are fewer and fewer corporations which profess such a narrowly conceived view of responsibility.

The next tier of the pyramid consists of legal regulations. Due to the enormous growth in the size of corporations and the increasing complexity of products and markets, a great increase can be observed in the regulation of corporate activities. Already, in earlier chapters, we saw indications and citations emphasizing the importance of regulators as stakeholders. Legally regulated responsibility is already part of ethical responsibility, since it reflects the norms anchored in society.

Ethical responsibility as a whole (tier 3) includes all the norms which are not legally anchored, but are sanctioned by society or societal groups.

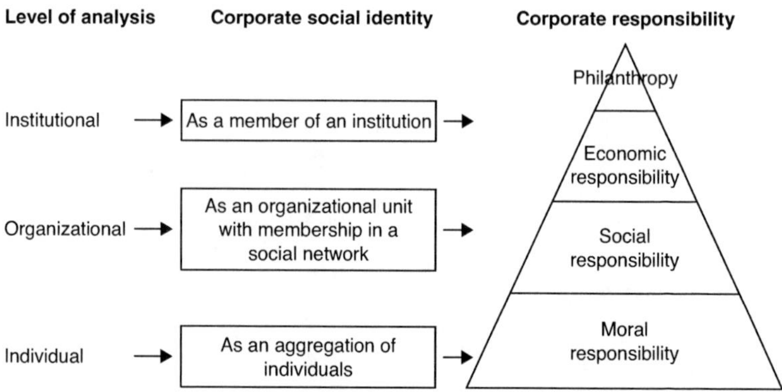

*Figure 10.2*   The pyramid turned 180°
*Source*: Based on Kang and Wood (1995).

The philanthropic responsibility, the last tier of the pyramid of responsibility and the next phase in the discussion, goes beyond legal and ethical responsibility. It includes corporate engagement which increases social welfare and is voluntary on the part of the corporation.

Another well-known concept turns the pyramid discussed above partly upside down (see Figure 10.2).

The basic assumption of the pyramid turned 180° is that corporations and society have a joint basis, and that is the moral responsibility of the individual. Therefore, a corporation may not be regarded as a purely economic entity detached from society. The basis is the philosopher Kant's famous maxim:

> It now follows of itself that in the order of ends the human being (and with him every rational being) is an *end in itself*, that is, can never be used merely as a means by anyone (not even by God) without being at the same time himself an end ... For, this moral law is based on the autonomy of his will, as a free will which, in accordance with its universal laws, must necessarily be able at the same time *to agree* to that to which it is to *subject* itself.[4]

According to this moral position, economic laws can never have priority if they injure the free will of human beings by seeing them as means rather than ends. This kind of problem is evident in the case of Enron. There were employees who reported that certain proceedings in the corporation were wrong. They were fired. After the scandal, there were employees who defended themselves with the argument that they did not report anything for fear of losing their jobs. Kant's maxim was severely violated here. In the meantime, cases of 'whistle blowers' are assuming more importance. For example, some corporations have telephone numbers through which employees can anonymously report any false practice they know about. Further tiers of responsibility can be built upon moral responsibility.

Deciding which of the two named concepts to follow in determining corporation responsibility is in the end a question of your personal value system. The first pyramid prescribes a basic economic premise; the second, a societal one. These value systems are topics to be openly addressed in your corporation, so that corporate action can be rightly understood by everyone.

In the following part of the chapter we are going to discuss another property-based value system which focuses on both the intellectual and material property of all relevant stakeholders.

## We are the owners

As previously discussed in Chapter 2, we assume an expanded understanding of property. Property is not only material and financial, but also a non-material asset like knowledge and experience. If a corporation accepts an inclusive principle of property as a part of their basic values, then two points of view need to be kept in mind in the context of corporate responsibility.

- In the corporate value-creation process, who are you considering and in what form?

Let us take another look at the example of Orange. Upon closing one of its call-centres, Orange became aware that such a decision should not have been made without taking the employees involved into consideration. Among the measures taken to correct the damage to this stakeholder relationship, an employee forum was introduced. This provided a means of including employees in important decision making. Today the forum is a link between staff and management.

Employees are informed in advance of decisions that affect them, and their input is considered in turn.

This example shows the importance of procedural justice. This form of justice accepts the fact that the corporation's value-creation process affects the benefit and risk potentials of its stakeholders. In our example, it is the employees of Orange who make their knowledge and experience – property in a broader sense – available to the corporation. According to the inclusive principle of property, they have the right to be included in the processes affecting this property. Justice is established through inclusion in the processes.

> Since 1976, Germany has a law regulating the participation of employees. It states that in a corporation with at least 2000 employees, half of the seats on the board of directors have to be reserved for employee representatives. The law also determines who can take a seat: one seat is for a managing employee, two to three seats are for union representatives, the other seats are for other employees.[5]

Table 10.1 gives some further examples of procedural justice. This can help you decide which stakeholders to include in your strategic planning for establishing procedural justice.

- Who is considered and in what way in value dissemination?

As already discussed, from a purely economic point of view, wealth dissemination considers primarily the shareholders. It is the discretion of management how much the shareholders are to be compensated, which is to say how much of the profit is to be distributed and how much retained (payout ratio). We have referred to this already in Chapter 3. If, as we have often demonstrated, other stakeholders have also made a significant contribution to the corporation's value-creation process then, on the basis of an extended understanding of property, these stakeholders should also be part of the value-dissemination process. This is called distributive justice. Determining the share of the individual stakeholders is again a matter of discretion. This is confirmed by one of our interview partners:

> 'I believe we pay good salaries when I compare with others, in fact particularly good salaries for regular employees and workers.

*Table 10.1*   Examples of procedural justice

| Stakeholder groups | Contribution to value creation of your corporation | Stakeholder engagement in processes |
| --- | --- | --- |
| Shareholders | Investments, financial risk bearers, capital expenditures | Voting rights at the general meeting (decision making) |
| Employees | Benefit of human capital; firm-specific investments | Employee forum for information and participation |
| Customers/ users | Risk of no longer receiving the desired products/services, e.g. on the basis of focusing on other product lines | Round-table on the development of products and services (possibly with lead users) |
| Suppliers | Risks based on firm-specific differentiation of your suppliers and their resulting dependence on your corporation | Inclusion in the process of developing products and services |
| Community/ society | Risk bearers based on environmental pollution and contamination | Inclusion of community representatives in the strategic sustainability advisory boards |
| Government | Tax reductions to improve the attractiveness of the location | Talks about the creation of new jobs in the community |

Here we are completely competitive. We also offer a high level of social security in regard to retirement and social plans. And we also don't pay any exaggerated salaries. The balance among customers, employees and investors is more or less right.'

Corporations, which at the time of their founding decided on value dissemination to a wide range of stakeholders, are usually state- or partially state-owned firms. As a result of high profits in 2007, one of the firms we analysed (an accident insurer with a public mandate) reduced the premiums of its clients by 5 per cent with the clear intention of letting the customers participate in its annual profit. Another analysed corporation with a public mandate (a bank) sets the amount of its public welfare spending so that the expenditure is visible both internally and externally, thus making its broad-based value dissemination intelligible to its stakeholders.

Among private corporations, Novo Nordisk, for example, accounts its value dissemination in detail. In its 'economic stakeholder model', the corporation itemizes how high the total salaries of employees are, how much it pays its suppliers for materials and services, how high the compound taxes are, and the amounts of dividend and interest payments to shareholders and investors.

We know of private insurance corporations, which grant their customers a premium bonus as the result of a good business year. Value in the form of a loyalty bonus is also given to long-term customers.

There are no limits to the ideas allowing employees and management to participate in the value creation of a corporation in general or in particular, as the following example shows.

**Example: Swiss Re**

For years Swiss Re has offered its employees an employee participating plan as an incentive programme. This programme is a share-savings plan with an option and a phantom element. It was introduced in May 2001, and 70 per cent of the employees took part in it. With this programme, Swiss Re seeks to encourage employees to own more Swiss Re shares, and thereby to participate in the corporation's success. In this way, Swiss Re hopes to encourage enterprising thinking, and an awareness of the most important factors in success, in its personnel. The employees agree to save part of their salary every month for a period of two years. Most of them are able to save up to 10 per cent of their salary. In this way, the base pay becomes an expression of individual performance. The better the performance, the more the employees earn and the more they can save with the programme. Swiss Re supports the employee investments worldwide with a 50 per cent contribution. With the saved amount, employees can buy a certain number of options, which can be converted into shares after two years. These shares have no retention period so employees can sell them if they choose. In 2002 this programme won the GEO Prize (Global Equity Organization). (www.geoawards.org)

Such plans influence the incentive of not only employees but also of managers. The employees are now part of those shareholders who demand a long-term view. This changes the perspectives and the values of top managers from a short-term to a long-term view. Since the employees as shareholders also bear a financial risk, the managers have to consider a broader view in their strategic thinking. They have to consider the employees in two categories of stakeholders: as employees and as owners. When they fail to do this, they discourage the employees, which in turn leads to lower performance. And in addition, the managers are motivated by their own participation in the programme.

Another interesting aspect to this perspective is that during wage negotiations in the fall of 2006, the employers of the German metal industry proactively declared that employees should be entitled to an appropriate share of the increased profits. One spoke of so-called investor wages, meaning a wage system whereby the employees could acquire ownership in the corporation.

In the meantime there are more and more examples of private corporations, and even those on the stock exchange, which allow for the dissemination of wealth among their strategically relevant stakeholders. A well-known example is Novo Nordisk. 'Understanding diabetes – Understanding people' is Novo Nordisk's vision statement, and this means that basically the customers as well as society should share in the wealth-dissemination process. Novo Nordisk naturally invests a great deal in commercially promising research and development in the area of diabetes. In addition to this research activity, Novo Nordisk has demonstrated a great deal of social engagement by supporting the World Diabetes Foundation (WDF), an international foundation for the improvement of diabetes care in developing countries, without the expectation of commercial benefit.

Another example is Porsche: the corporation did exceptionally well in 2007 and gave its employees a share in the profits. All full-time employees received a bonus of €5200. The previous year Porsche had awarded its employees a special payment of €3800. The homepage of Porsche's website justified the bonus in the following way:

The Board of Directors and the Labour Council are of the opinion that the successful effort to increase the productivity, flexibility and quality of the corporation – and to secure its position – must be worthwhile for everyone concerned. Therefore Porsche is again

*Table 10.2*   Examples of distributive justice

| Stakeholder groups | Contribution to value creation of your corporation | Participation in value dissemination |
| --- | --- | --- |
| Shareholders | Investments, financial risk bearers, capital expenditures | Share of residual profit, Shareholder Value |
| Employees | Benefit of human capital; firm-specific investments | Contributions to further training, bonus system, incentive programme, etc. |
| Suppliers | Risks based on firm-specific differentiation and the resulting dependence on your corporation | Compensation for supplier risks and knowledge contribution |
| Joint-venture partners and alliances | Supplementing resources, stabilizing market position | Benefit and profit participation; compensation for alliance risks |
| Community/ society | Risk bearers on the basis of environmental pollution and contamination | Corporation philanthropy, financial and non-financial compensation for risks |
| Non-governmental organizations (NGOs) | Information on societal risks | Scientific exchange, cost of transparency |

distributing a share of the profits to its highly motivated and hard-working employees, who with their dedication continue to be the backbone of the positive development.[6]

In 2007 at Swiss (the airline), a model for allowing employees to participate in the corporation's success was introduced: 'The model provides for higher participation depending on the corporation's rate of return. For a margin of 5 percent, an employee receives 3 percent of his gross annual salary. The maximum is 10 percent with a margin of 12 percent.'[7]

Table 10.2 gives you an overview of further examples of distributive justice. These examples can also give you an idea of how to structure distributive justice in your corporation.

## How responsibility translates into hard currency

As we have already seen in the last chapter, research has shown that sustainable engagement in the economic, societal and ecological areas

of stakeholder relations can have a verifiable, positive influence on the financial success of a corporation. In particular, more innovative solutions are possible by including strategically relevant stakeholders in the business processes, which enhance the three licences (licence to operate, compete and innovate). The consideration of strategically

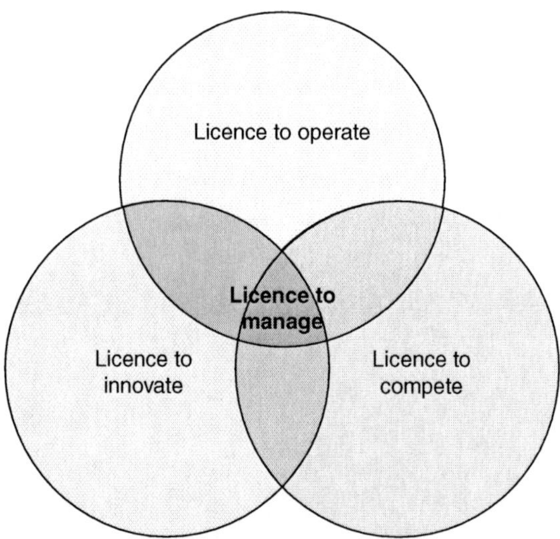


*Figure 10.3*   The three corporate licences

relevant stakeholders in the value-dissemination process ensures and increases the long-term motivation of stakeholders to continue to commit themselves and support the corporation.

The resulting motto is therefore:

**The corporation is credible due to its comprehensive corporate responsibility. The licence to manage is achieved by the executive staff when they are able to bring together the three corporate licences: licence to innovate, licence to compete and licence to operate.**

The following questions are therefore relevant for you:

1. What is my understanding of corporate responsibility in my corporation?
2. How do I bind the strategically relevant stakeholders in a strategic developmental process?
3. How are the strategically relevant stakeholders considered in the value-dissemination process?

4. Have I brought together the licence to innovate, to compete and to operate so that I warrant my licence to manage and am credible as an executive staff member?

## Notes

1  ABB (2002).
2  20Minuten (2007), p. 16.
3  Friedman (1962), p. 133.
4  Kant (1996), p. 245f (italics in original).
5  Förderland (2006).
6  Porsche (2007).
7  CASHdaily (2007a), p. 2.

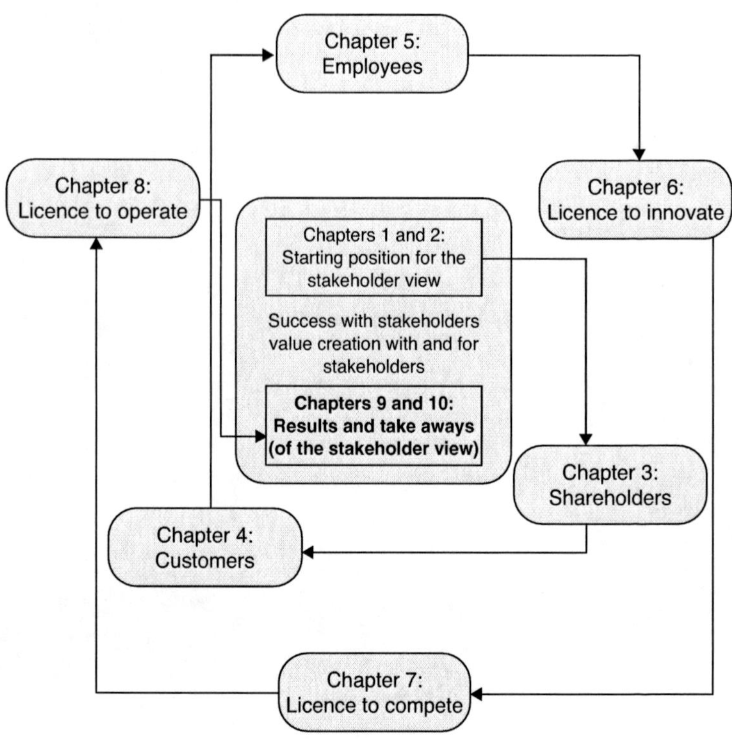

Chapter 5:
Employees
Chapter 8:
Licence to operate
Chapter 6:
Licence to innovate
Chapters 1 and 2:
Starting position for the
stakeholder view
Success with stakeholders
value creation with and for
stakeholders
Chapters 9 and 10:
Results and take aways
(of the stakeholder view)
Chapter 3:
Shareholders
Chapter 4:
Customers
Chapter 7:
Licence to compete

# Take aways

If after reading this book you are interested in finding ways to implement stakeholder oriented management, then the following ten principles, and the working through of the questions associated with them, should be useful.

1. You are part of a complex and interrelated world, and therefore need a comprehensive strategic management concept: The stakeholder view provides the key.

   - Which kinds of events from the standpoint of the history of my corporation are important for future stakeholder relations?
   - What and how have I and my corporation learned from them?
   - Are there core values in my corporation that encourage a stakeholder orientation?

2. Find out who your corporation's most important stakeholders are, and when they are beneficial and when harmful.

   - Who are the most important stakeholders for my corporation?
   - Which are the benefit and risk potentials of these stakeholders?
   - What do these potentials mean for my core stakeholders, namely the shareholders, customers and employees?
   - What contribution do these potentials make to my corporation's strategy?
   - How should the stakeholder orientation be communicated?

3. Integrate your shareholders into corporate activities, thus making them real stakeholders.

   - Which are the most important shareholder groups of my corporation, and what are their interests, commitments and potentials?
   - How do my essential shareholders judge the benefit and risk potential of my other strategically relevant stakeholders?
   - How sustainable or how long term is the nature of my business? Which shareholders have a similar view of the business?
   - How attractive is my business for the desired category of investors?
   - What might communication with the desired investors look like concretely in my case?

4. Learning from customers is strategically relevant, since their knowledge and experience may be valuable for your corporation.

   - Is the paramount importance of the customers as strategic stake-holders recognized in my corporation, and not just preached but also practised?
   - Which categories of customers are to be distinguished, in order to have a sufficiently differentiated overall picture? What are the benefit and risk potentials of these customer segments?
   - What forms and methods of learning are appropriate in asso-ciation with customers? Are opportunities for collaborative learning widely used in my corporation?
   - Are there typical lead users in my business who could contribute to my strategies and innovations?

5. Employees are important knowledge bearers. Make use of their knowledge relevant for your corporation.

   - What are the personnel categories which are decisive for the strategic success of my corporation?
   - What are the benefit and risk potentials of the various personnel categories?
   - How do I see employee potential in contrast to the current highly propagated cost reduction tactics? To what extent am I

willing to resist this pressure or to make long term investments in the knowledge potential of my employees?
- How favourable are the conditions in my corporation to use, propagate and promote the knowledge of my employees?

6. Develop your core competences with the participation of your stakeholders in order to strengthen your 'licence to innovate.'

   - What are the current and future core competences of my corporation?
   - What strategic resources are especially relevant for maintaining my 'licence to innovate'?
   - Which of my stakeholders have these resources at their disposal?
   - How can I establish a relationship with these stakeholders?

7. Position your corporation effectively in the stakeholder network in order to insure your 'licence to compete'.

   - What does my stakeholder network look like in general, and in relation to the most important strategic projects?
   - Do I have an *agent provocateur* in my stakeholder network, and how do I deal with him?
   - Which benefits and risk potentials can I gain or avoid through careful positioning in the stakeholder network?
   - How can I further awareness of a network of stakeholder relations in my corporation?
   - Which of my stakeholders exercise a variety of functions; what are the resulting opportunities and risks?

8. Take into consideration the social and political stakeholders of your corporation, and their needs and expectations. They influence your 'licence to operate'.

   - What are the societal needs and expectations which my corporation could be confronted with?
   - Which social and political stakeholders are relevant regarding my strategic issues?
   - To what extent do the values of my strategically relevant social and political stakeholders differ from that of the corporation?

- How is my corporation represented in the public domain regarding societal concerns?

9. Increase the transparency and sustainability of your activities and speak about them with your stakeholders.

   - What does sustainability mean in my corporation? Does it include the four basic principles of property, competition, legitimacy, and balance?
   - How is my concept of sustainability reflected in the goals I set?
   - What indicators or instruments do I use in order to advance the sustainability of my value creation processes and to make this transparent for my strategically relevant stakeholders?

10. Corporate responsibility involves including the stakeholders consciously in the value creation process. This contributes significantly to sustainable strategic success.

    - What is my understanding of corporate responsibility in my corporation?
    - How can I include my strategically relevant stakeholders in a strategic development process?
    - What consideration is taken of my strategically relevant stakeholders in the value creation process?

We would like to end our book with the motto:

**Value creation for and with stakeholders**

# Appendix I: Research Project 'Good Practices of Stakeholder View'

This book is primarily based on the findings of our research project 'Good Practices of Stakeholder View of Strategy'. For many years the research group, under the leadership of the authors Sybille Sachs and Edwin Rühli, has concerned itself with the role of the corporation in today's society and in particular with stakeholder management. The research team included several Ph.D candidates, who were employed either as research assistants or in the firms that were part of the project. Shortly before this, the third author, Isabelle Kern, completed her dissertation on 'The Suitability of Topic Maps Tools for Knowledge Creation with Stakeholders'. We would like to thank all the current and former members of the research team for their valuable work: Dominic Käslin, Marc Maurer, Veronika Mittnacht, René Nicolodi, Irène Perrin, Daniel Peter, Torsten Schäfer, Ruth Schmitt, Stefan Schuppisser, Georges Ulrich, Mark Veser.

The research project was and is supported by the University of Applied Sciences for Business Administration (Zürich), the SLOAN Foundation (USA), the European Academy for Business in Society (EABIS), the Swiss National Science Foundation, the association Forum Stakeholder View, the Federal Department of Foreign Affairs (DFA), the Commission for Technology and Innovation (CTI), the Federal Office of Education and Science (OES) and Ecoscientia, all in Switzerland. It is embedded in various national and international networks.

The forerunner project 'Redefining the Corporation' was done primarily together with the two American professors Lee Preston (Maryland University) and James Post (Boston University). On the basis of three longitudinal case studies of the corporations Shell, Motorola and Cummins, the comprehensive management approach 'Stakeholder View of Strategy' was established. A book (*Redefining the Corporation: Stakeholder Management and Organizational Wealth,*

Stanford University Press, 2002) as well as several publications in high-ranking, international journals followed. In the fall of 2002, the new research project 'Good Practices of Stakeholder View of Strategy' was initiated with a conference of the association Forum Stakeholder View at the Swiss Re Centre for Global Dialogue. In June 2007 it was concluded with another conference at the same location and with the publication of this book.

## Goals of the project

Within the framework of the project, six comparative case studies were carried out, in which the following goals were focused on:

- Analysing examples of the development and implementation of the Stakeholder View in practice
- Devising tools for the Stakeholder View
- Developing the 'Stakeholder View of Strategy' framework further.

In so doing, the following research questions were investigated:

- How do corporations learn to develop a comprehensive Stakeholder View?
- How is the Stakeholder View of Strategy integrated into the structure and culture of the corporation?
- How is stakeholder-oriented reporting done, and how is the success of stakeholder oriented management judged?

## Methodology

The above-mentioned research questions were investigated with comparative case studies. Corporations with a certain amount of stakeholder orientation were analysed with a comparative qualitative case research method.

In the beginning of each case study, a qualitative content analysis of the documents of the firms was made. Afterwards, on the basis of this knowledge, interviews with top management were held, which were again analysed according to content as above. The insights of this analysis and that of the documents were compared and summarized in a report for the respective firms. Appendix II contains the essential findings of these case studies. The stakeholder-oriented behaviour of the individual firms provides a source of additional stimulation.

In a next step, firms in the same industry were compared in order to determine similarities and differences. We chose two industries to compare:

- Telecommunications with the firms Orange, Sunrise and Swisscom
- Financial Services with the firms Suva, Swiss Re and ZKB.

Finally, there is an analysis of the similarities and differences irrespective of industry.

Should you want to know more about the conclusions or the methodology, we refer you to the following publications and conference reports:

## Authors' papers and publications

### 2008

Sachs, S., Rühli, E. and Kern, I. (2008) 'The Globalization as Challenge for the Stakeholder Management', Paper presented at the Annual Meeting of the Academy of Management (AoM), Anaheim, California.

Sachs, S. and Maurer, M. (forthcoming) 'Toward Dynamic Corporate Stakeholder Responsibility', *Journal of Business Ethics*.

Sachs, S., Groth, H. and Schmitt, R. (2008) 'Understanding the Stakeholders' Perception of a Common Strategic Issue to Manage a Stakeholder Network: A Single Case Study in the Pharmaceutical Industry', Paper presented at the Annual Meeting of the International Association for Business and Society (IABS), Tampere, Finland.

Sachs, S., Schmitt, R. and Perrin, I. (2008) 'Stakeholder Value Management System', Paper presented at Annual Meeting of the International Association for Business and Society (IABS), Tampere, Finland.

### 2007

Kern, I., Sachs, S. and Rühli, E. (2007) 'How Stakeholder Relations Pay Off by Maintaining the Licence to Operate: A Comparative Case Study of the Swiss Telecommunications Industry', *Corporate Governance: International Journal for Business in Society*, 7(4): 446–54.

Sachs, S. and Groth, H. (2007) 'Aufwachen, bevor es zu spät ist: Die Schweizer Pharmaindustrie und ihre Stakeholderbeziehungen', *IO New Management*, April 2007.

Sachs, S., Käslin, D. and Mittnacht, V. (2007) 'Methodology at the Crossroads: Qualitative and Quantitative Analysis of Comparative Case Studies', Annual Meeting of the International Association for Business and Society (IABS), Florence, Italy.

Sachs, S. and Rühli, E. (2007) 'The Global Governance as Challenge for the Strategic Management', Paper presented at the 6th Annual Colloquium of the European Academy of Business in Society (EABIS), Barcelona, Spain.

Sachs, S., Rühli, E. and Käslin, D. (2007) 'Methodology for Inter- and Intra-Industry Case Comparison in the Good Practices Stakeholder View Research Project', Paper presented at the International Association for Business and Society (IABS) in Florence, Italy 2007.

Sachs, S., Rühli, E. and Kern, I. (2007) *Lizenz zum Managen. Mit Stakeholdern zum Erfolg: Herausforderungen und Good Practices*, Bern: Haupt Verlag.

Sachs, S., Rühli, E. and Kern, I. (2007) 'Stakeholder Relations as a Corporate Core to Operate, Compete and Innovate', Proceedings of the Annual Meeting of the International Association for Business and Society (IABS), Florence, Italy: 470–75.

Sachs, S., Rühli, E. and Mittnacht, V. (2007) 'How Stakeholder Relations Impact Corporate Strategy – An Empirical Investigation', Proceedings of the Annual Meeting of the International Association for Business and Society (IABS), Florence, Italy: 476–81.

Sachs, S., Rühli, E. and Mittnacht, V. (2007) 'Inter- and Intra-Industry Comparison of the Strategic Stakeholder Management in the Telecommunication and Financial Services Industry of Switzerland', Paper presented at the International Association for Business and Society (IABS) in Florence, Italy 2007.


## 2006

Sachs, S. and Käslin, D. (2006) 'Qualitative Comparative Methods for Multiple Case Studies: An Empirical Investigation for Strategic Stakeholder Management', Proceedings of the Annual Conference of the International Association for Business and Society (IABS) in Mérida, Mexico: 316–21.

Sachs, S., Rühli, E. and Maurer, M. (2006) 'Toward a Stakeholder Orientation in Strategic Management', Paper presented at the Annual Meeting of the Academy of Management, Atlanta.

Sachs, S. and Maurer, M. (2006) 'From Corporate Social Responsibility Toward Corporate Stakeholder Responsibility', Paper presented at the Annual Meeting of the Academy of Management, Atlanta.

Sachs, S., Maurer, M., Rühli, E. and Hoffmann, R. (2006) 'Corporate Social Responsibility from a Stakeholder View Perspective: CSR Implementation by a Swiss Mobile Telecommunications Provider', *Corporate Governance: International Journal for Business in Society*, 6(4): 506–15.

Sachs, S., Rühli, E. and Maurer, M. (2006) 'The Effects of Liberalization and Privatization on Former Monopolist's Stakeholder Interactions', Paper presented at the Politeia Conference in Milan, Italy.

Kern, I. (2006) 'Topic Maps for Knowledge Creation with Stakeholders', *Proceedings of the 7th European Conference on Knowledge Management (ECKM)*, Budapest, Hungary: ECKM, pp. 260–67.


## 2005

Sachs, S. (2005) 'Die Bedeutung der Stakeholder für Fachhochschulen', in Dürsteler, U. and Knecht, H. (eds.), *Bildungsökonomische Herausforderungen der Fachhochschulen*, Vol. 1: pp. 35–55.

Sachs, S. and Kern, I. (2005) 'The Contribution of the Stakeholder View of the Knowledge-Creation Framework of Nonaka and Takeuchi', *Proceedings of the Annual Conference of the International Association for Business and Society (IABS)*, Sonoma, California: IABS, pp. 337–41.

Sachs, S. and Maurer, M. (2005) 'Implementing the Stakeholder View – Learning Process towards a Changed Stakeholder Orientation', *Journal of Corporate Citizenship*, (17): 93–107.

Sachs, S. and M. Maurer (2005) 'A Hermeneutic Classificatory Content Analysis for Good Practices Stakeholder View Project', Working Paper.

Sachs, S. and Maurer, M. (2005) 'Toward a Comprehensive View on Corporate Stakeholder Responsibility', International Sustainability Conference in Basle, Switzerland.

Sachs, S. and Rühli, E. (2005) 'Changing Managers' Values towards a Broader Stakeholder Orientation', *Corporate Governance: International Journal for Business in Society*, 5(2): 89–98.

Sachs, S. and Rühli, E. (2005) 'Practical Issues in Implementing the Stakeholder View as a Core Competence', in Sanchez, R. and Heene, A. (eds), *Competence Perspectives on Resources, Stakeholders and Renewal*, Advances in Applied Business Strategy Series, Vol. 9.

Sachs, S., Rühli, E. and Mittnacht, V. (2005) 'A CSR Framework Due to Multiculturalism: The Swiss Re Case', *Corporate Governance: International Journal for Business in Society*, 5(3): 52–60.

Sachs, S. and Veser, M. (2005) 'Normative Foundation of Stakeholder View – an International Perspective', Paper presented at the Annual Meeting of the Society of Business Ethics in Honolulu, Hawaii.

## 2004

Rühli, E. (2004) '100 Jahre BWL an der Universität Zürich: Die Entwicklung der Betriebswirtschaftslehre (BWL) zur heutigen akademischen Disziplin an der Universität Zürich', in *Die Unternehmung*, Vol. 3, No. 4: 191–5.

Sachs, S. and Rühli, E. (2004) 'Stakeholder View: A Case Research', Paper presented at the Academy of Management (AoM), New Orleans.

Sachs, S., Rühli, E. and Mittnacht, V. (2004) 'A CSR Framework due to Multiculturalism: The Swiss Re Case. Corporate Governance', Paper presented at the Third Annual Colloquium of the European Academy of Business in Society (EABIS), Ghent, Belgium.

Sachs, S. and Maurer, M. (2004) 'Implementing the stakeholder view: Learning processes towards a broader stakeholder orientation', Paper presented at the Annual Conference of the International Association for Business and Society (IABS), Jackson Hole, USA.

## 2003

Rühli, E. and Sachs, S. (2003) 'Der Stakeholder Ansatz: Ein umfassendes Framework des Strategischen Managements', in Matzler, K., Pechlaner, H., Renzl, B. (eds), *Werte schaffen: Perspektiven einer stakeholderorientierten Unternehmensführung*, Wiesbaden: Gabler Verlag, pp. 49–71.

Sachs, S. and Munshi, N. (2003) 'Interrelatedness and Value Creation in Firm-Stakeholder Networks', Paper presented at the Annual Conference of the Academy of Management (AoM), Seattle.

Sachs, S. and Rühli, E. (2003) 'Implementing the Stakeholder View – an Empirical Investigation', Paper presented at the Meeting of the Academy of Management (AoM), Denver.

Sachs, S, Rühli, E. and Peter, D. (2003) 'Implementing the Stakeholder View – Changing Managers' Values to Enhance Strategic Success', Paper presented at the Annual Conference of the International Association for Business and Society (IABS), Rotterdam, NL.

Sachs, S. and Rühli, E. (2003) 'Case Research in Stakeholder Management', Paper presented at the Second Annual Colloquium of the European Academy of Business in Society (EABIS), Copenhagen, DK.

# Appendix II: Information on Case Study Firms

## Corporations in the area of financial services

*Table A.1*   General information Suva

| Corporation and legal form | Swiss Accident Insurance Company, independent company under public law ('Suva') |
|---|---|
| **Corporate governance** | 100 % ownership by the companies insured and their employees |
| **Market position** | Most important institution of obligatory accident insurance in Switzerland. It insures employees against occupational accidents and illness, and non-occupational accidents, as a partial monopoly |
| **Turnover** | CHF 7,021 Mio. (2007) |
| **Employees** | 2,800 (2007) |
| **Declared profit** | CHF 355 Mio. (2007) |
| **Founded** | 1912, start of operation 1918 |
| **Most important stakeholders** | • Customers<br>• Employees<br>• Federal government (Council, Parliament, Departments)<br>• Social partners<br>• Physicians |
| **Special features of stakeholder orientation** | Suva has a strong stakeholder orientation. Suva's activities are embedded in a complex stakeholder network, which has a long tradition and is very important to the firm. |
| **Wake-up calls** | Industrialization of the society brought about the founding of Suva in 1912. |

*Table A.2*   General information Swiss Re

| | |
|---|---|
| **Corporation and legal form** | Swiss Reinsurance Corporation ('Swiss Re') |
| **Corporate governance** | A corporation traded on SWX Zürich und virt-x with a broad base of shareholders. 58.43 % of the shares are in the hands of institutional investors. |
| **Market position** | World market-leader in the reinsurance industry. Worldwide provider of products in the segment of life and health, property and liability, as well as financial services with resource oriented corporate strategy. |
| **Turnover** | CHF 42,874 Mio. (2007) |
| **Employees** | 11,700 (2007) |
| **Declared profit** | CHF 4,162 Mio. (2007) |
| **Founded** | 1863 |
| **Most important stakeholders** | • Shareholders<br>• Employees<br>• Customers<br>• Regulators |
| **Special features of stakeholder orientation** | Swiss Re has a high stakeholder awareness and sees the relationship with strategic stakeholders from a value creation perspective. |
| **Wake-up calls** | Founding of Swiss Re |

*Table A.3*   General information Zurich Cantonal Bank

| | |
|---|---|
| **Corporation and legal form** | Zurich Cantonal Bank, independent institution under cantonal public law ('ZKB') |
| **Corporate governance** | 100 % ownership by the canton of Zürich |
| **Market position** | Third largest bank of Switzerland with activities in all areas of universal banking. Market oriented strategy, aiming at continuity and stability in a state of flux. |
| **Turnover (operating revenue)** | CHF 2,100 Mio. (2007) |
| **Employees** | 4,446 (2007) |
| **Declared profit** | CHF 843 Mio. (2007) |
| **Founded** | 1870 |
| **Most important stakeholders** | • Customers<br>• Employees<br>• Owners<br>• Suppliers<br>• Society<br>• Politics |

*(Continued)*

*Table A.3*   (Continued)

| | |
|---|---|
| **Special features of stakeholder orientation** | Since the founding of ZKB, stakeholder relations are actively cultivated, whereby the principles for associating with priority stakeholders result from the performance related mandate of the bank. Customers, employees and in part the society are seen as value creation factors. |
| **Wake-up calls** | Founding ZKB by the Council of Canton Zürich |

## Corporations from the area of telecommunications

*Table A.4*   General information Orange

| | |
|---|---|
| **Corporation and legal form** | Orange Switzerland Inc. |
| **Corporate governance** | 100 % subsidiary of Orange Inc., a corporation of the France Télécom |
| **Market position** | Nr. 3 in the Swiss telecommunication market, mobile communication provider with niche strategy |
| **Turnover** | CHF 1,339 Mio. (2007) |
| **Employees** | 1,244 (2007) |
| **Declared profit** | CHF 395 Mio. (2004; no information available after 2004) |
| **Founded** | 1998 |
| **Most important stakeholders** | • Customers<br>• Shareholders<br>• Employees<br>• Regulators<br>• Residents near antennas |
| **Special features of stakeholder orientation** | Orange has a strong stakeholder orientation and sees 'Corporate Responsibility' as a core value. However due to the market situation and the high profit expectations of the owners, there is cost pressure which influences the stakeholder orientation. |
| **Wake-up calls** | • Market entry<br>• Cooling of the market, and subsequent restructuring and personnel cutbacks |

*Table A.5*  General information Sunrise

| | |
|---|---|
| **Corporation and legal form** | TDC Switzerland Co ('Sunrise') |
| **Corporate governance** | 100 % subsidiary of TDC Group (Denmark) |
| **Market position** | Only alternative to previous monopoly – challenger<br>Nr. 2 in Swiss telecommunication market.<br>Full-service-provider with cost-leader-strategy. |
| **Turnover** | CHF 1,949 Mio. (2007) |
| **Employees** | 2,500 (2007) |
| **Declared profit** | CHF 170 Mio. (2007) |
| **Founded** | 2000 (forerunner companies Sunrise and diAx founded 1996 ) |
| **Most important stakeholders** | • Customers<br>• Employees<br>• Media<br>• Regulators<br>• Society<br>• Shareholders<br>• Business partners<br>• Politics |
| **Special features of stakeholder orientation** | After a case to case approach at the beginning, today a broader concentration on stakeholders (Corporate Citizenship). |
| **Wake-up calls** | • Founding and start-up<br>• Mobile telephone system – licensing<br>• Antenna topic for diAx (after 1998) |

*Table A.6*  General information Swisscom

| | |
|---|---|
| **Corporation and legal form** | Swisscom Inc. |
| **Corporate governance** | A corporation traded on SWX Zürich and NYSE New York. 62,5 % of the shares are owned by the Swiss Federal Government. |
| **Market position** | Nr. 1 in the Swiss telecommunication market |
| **Turnover** | CHF 11,089 Mio. (2007) |
| **Employees** | 19,844 (2007) |
| **Declared profit** | CHF 2,071 Mio. (2007) |
| **Founded** | 1998 (forerunner company PTT founded 1852) |

*(Continued)*

*Table A.6*   (Continued)

| Most important stakeholders | • Customers<br>• Employees<br>• Shareholders<br>• State as multifunctional stakeholder |
| --- | --- |
| Special features of stakeholder orientation | Swisscom has a generally highly developed stakeholder awareness. The existing stakeholder relationships provided Swisscom with a sustainable competitive advantage, which is hardly imitable by the competition. |
| Wake-up calls | • Founding of the forerunner institution as a monopoly<br>• Liberalization of the market and the subsequent founding of today's partially privatized Swisscom |

## Corporations from the area of pharmaceuticals

*Table A.7*   General information Pfizer Switzerland

| Corporation and legal form | Pfizer Switzerland Inc. |
| --- | --- |
| Corporate governance | 100 % subsidiary of Pfizer Inc. USA |
| Market position | Swiss market leader |
| Turnover | 48,418 Mio $ (Pfizer Inc.) (2007) |
| Employees | 260 (Switzerland) (2007) |
| Declared profit | 8,144 Mio $ (Pfizer Inc.) (2007) |
| Founded | 1959 (in Switzerland) |
| Most important stakeholders | • Physicians<br>• Health insurances<br>• Patients<br>• Media<br>• Pharma Industry |
| Special features of stakeholder orientation | Pfizer's relationships with stakeholders are strictly regulated. Pfizer has intense relationships with physicians, but not with other stakeholders, due to regulatory constraints. |
| Wake-up calls | • Claims from different stakeholders, mainly concerning the problem of cost control<br>• New challenges regarding Corporate Citizenship and Stakeholder relationships. |

# References

20Minuten (2007), 161 Mio Dollar zur "Pension"', *20 Minuten*, Zurich, 1 November 2007.

ABB (2002) ABB einigt sich mit Barnevik und Lindahl, www02.abb.com/GLOBAL/ABBZH/abbzh250.nsf/99ad595c32e0c2d9c12566e1000a4540/d938498e6b9694cfc1256b78005090f3/$FILE/german.pdf#search=%22ABB%20einigt%20sich%20mit%20Barnevik%20und%20Lindahl%22. (14 July 2006).

ABB (2007) Das Programm "Generations": ABB setzt auf den Mix der Generationen, www.abb.de/cawp/deabb204/db80f2b49c67dedcc125727400399ee9.aspx (20 November 2007).

Barney, J. (1991) 'Firm Resources and Sustained Competitive Advantage', *Journal of Management*, Vol. 17, No. 1: 99–120.

Bartz, T. (2008) Dossier Citibank steht vor dem Verkauf, *Financial Times Deutschland*, Frankfurt, 18 May 2008.

BASF (2007) BASF to Delist from New York Stock Exchange, www.corporate.basf.com/en/investor/news/mitteilungen/pm.htm?pmid=2792&id=V00-NzegIBB.Cbcp3dn (8 October 2007).

BBC (2006a) Sarbanes-Oxley 'Hurting the US', http://news.bbc.co.uk/2/hi/business/4949386.stm (15 January 2008).

BBC (2006b) US Fears Firms Listing Overseas, http://news.bbc.co.uk/2/hi/business/6158603.stm (15 January 2008).

Blowfield, M. and Googins, B. K. (2006) Step Up: A Call for Business Leadership in Society: CEOs Examine Role of Business in the 21st Century, www.cpi.cam.ac.uk/pdf/BLIS%20final%20report.pdf (4 October 2007).

Bogle, J. C. (2005) *The Battle for the Soul of Capitalism*, New Haven and London: Yale University Press.

Brooker, K. (2006) How Pepsi Outgunned Coke, *Fortune*, 1 February 2006.

Business-Ethics (2007) Business Ethics 100 Best Corporate Citizens 2007, www.business-ethics.com/node/75 (2 November 2007).

Carroll, A. B. (1991) 'The Pyramid of Corporate Social Responsibility: Toward the Moral Management of Organizational Stakeholders', *Business Horizons*, Vol. 34, No. 1991: 39–48.

CASHdaily (2007a) Die Swiss im Steigflug gibt sich generös, *CASHdaily*, Zürich, 9 November 2007.

CASHdaily (2007b) Gläserne Staatsfirmen, *CASHdaily*, Zürich, 17 September 2007.

Cassingham, R. (2006) The 2005 True Stella Awards Winners www.stellaawards.com/2005.html (30 March 2006).

CBG (2005) Coordination gegen BAYER-Gefahren, www.cbgnetwork.org/872.html, www.cbgnetwork.org/1465.html, www.cbgnetwork.org/1517.html (1 November 2006).

Citizen Works (2002): The Corporate Scandal Sheet, www.citizenworks.org/enron/corp-scandal.php (8 October 2007).

CNN (2005) A \$400 Bet on Google?, http://money.cnn.com/2005/07/22/technology/google_analysis/index.htm (30 April 2006).

CNN (2007) Fisher-Price Recalls 1M toys, www.cnn.com/2007/US/08/01/toy.recall.ap/index.html (21 November 2007).

Collins, C., Ericksen, J. and Allen, M. (2006) *Human Resource Management Practices and Firm Performance in Small Businesses*, Research Report on Phase 4 of the Cornell University / Gevity Institute Study – Financial Impact, www.gevityinstitute. com/library/cornell_reports/cornell2_full_report.pdf.

Cusumano, M. A., Mylonadis, Y. and Rosenbloom, R. S. (1992) 'Strategic Maneuvering and Mass-Market Dynamics: The Triumph of VHS over Beta', *The Business History Review*, Vol. 66, No. 1: 51–94.

Deloitte, Euronext and CSR-Europe (2003) *Investing in Responsible Business. The 2003 Survey of European Fund Managers, Financial Analysts and Investor Relations Officers*, Brussels: CSR Europe.

Educating for Justice (EFJ) (2004) *Campaigns*, http://www.educatingforjustice. org/stopnikesweatshops.htm (1 November 2007).

EIRO (1999) Privatisation and Industrial Relations, www.eurofound.europa.eu/eiro/1999/12/study/TN9912201S.htm

EIRO (2001a) Arbeitsbedingter Stress und die Arbeitsbeziehungen, www.eiro.eurofound.ie/2001/11/study/tn0111149s.html

EIRO (2001b) Danone Reignites Controversy over Redundancies in Profitable Firms, www.eiro.eurofound.eu.int/2001/02/feature/fr0102133f.html

EIRO (2001c) Globalisation Blamed for Restructuring at Danone and Marks & Spencer, www.eiro.eurofound.eu.int/2001/04/feature/fr0104147f.html

EIRO (2002) Corporate Governance Systems and the Nature of Industrial Restructuring, www.eiro.eurofound.ie/2002/09/study/tn0209101s.html

Ethos (2006) Umwelt- und Sozialreporting der Schweizer Unternehmen, Genf, www.ethosfund.ch/upload/publication/p40d_060201_umwelt_und_sozialreporting_der_schweizer_unternehmen.pdf

Eurosif (2006) *European SRI Study 2006*, www.forum-ng.de/upload/pdf/pdf-Studien-extern/Eurosif_SRIStudy_2006_complete.pdf (6 November 2007).

Forbes (2007) Bayer Intends to Delist from New York Stock Exchange, www.forbes.com/businesswire/feeds/businesswire/2007/09/05/businesswire20070904006350r1.html (8 October 2007).

Förderland (2006) Mitbestimmungsgesetz von 1976 – In die Jahre gekommen, www.foerderland.de/907+M5175b21545e.0.html (11 January 2008).

Freeman, R. E. (1984) *Strategic Management: A Stakeholder Approach*, Boston, MA: Pitman.

Friedman, M. (1962) *Capitalism and Freedom*, Chicago and London: University of Chicago Press.

GfK (2006) Kaum Vertrauen in Politiker, GFK Custom Research Worldwide, www.gfk.com/group/press_information/press_releases/new/00841/index.de. html (7 November 2007).

Gibson, C. H. (1973) 'Volvo Increases Productivity Through Job Enrichment', *California Management Review*, Vol. 15, No. 4: 64–6.

Global-Exchange (2007) Nike Campaign, www.globalexchange.org/campaigns/ sweatshops/nike/ (1 November 2007).

Grant, R. M. (1996) 'Toward a Knowledge-Based Theory of the Firm', *Strategic Management Journal*, Vol. 17, (Special Issue Winter): 109–22.

Grote, G. and Staffelbach, B. (2006) *Schweizer HR-Barometer 2006*, Zürich: Verlag Neue Zürcher Zeitung.

Guest, D. E., Michie, J., Conway, N. and Sheehan, M. (2003) 'Human Resource Management and Corporate Performance in the UK', *British Journal of Industrial Relations*, Vol. 41 (June): 291–314.

Gyllenhammar, P. (1973) 'Volvo's Solution to the Blue Collar Blues', *Business and Society Review*, Vol., (Fall): 50–3.

Hall, R. (1992) 'The Strategic Analysis of Intangible Assets', *Strategic Management Journal*, Vol. 13, No. 2: 135–44.

Hall, R. (1993) 'A Framework Linking Intangible Resources and Capabilities to Sustainable Competitive Advantage', *Strategic Management Journal*, Vol. 14, No. 8: 607–18.

Hauck, W. and Ross, T. L. (1988) 'Expanded Teamwork at Volvo Through Performance Gainsharing', *Industrial Management*, Vol. 30, No. July–August: 17–20.

Herstatt, C., Lüthje, C. and Lettl, C. (2002) 'Wie fortschrittliche Kunden zu Innovationen stimulieren', *Harvard Businessmanager*, Vol. 1: 2–9.

IBM (2006) *Expanding the Horizon: Global CEO Study 2006*, www.ibm.com/ibm/ ideasfromibm/us/enterprise/mar27/ceo_study.html (2 November 2007).

IPCC (2007) *Climate Change 2007*, www.ipcc.ch/ (3 November 2007).

Jaruzelski, B. and Dehoff, K. (2007) 'The Customer Connection: The Global Innovation 1000', *Strategy + Business*, Vol. Winter, No. 49: 69–83.

Kalbreier, L., Prettre, H. and Zürcher, A. (2007) *Stocks with Family Influence*, Global Investor, Credit Suisse, Issue 01, January 2007: 49–51.

Kang, Y.-C. and Wood, D. J. (1995) 'Before-Profit Social Responsibility: Turning the Economic Paradigm Upside Down', *Proceedings of the Sixth Annual Meeting of the International Association for Business and Society (IABS), Vienna*, 408–18.

Kant, I. (1996) *The Critique of Practical Reason*, Cambridge: Cambridge University Press.

Leitner, K.-H. (2001) 'Intangible Resources and Firm Performance: Empirical Evidence from Austrian SMEs', 16th Nordic Academy of Management Meeting, Uppsala, Finland.

Locke, R. M. (2002) *The Promise and Perils of Globalization: The Case of Nike*, 50th Anniversary of the Sloan School of Management, http://web.mit.edu/ polisci/research/locke/nikepaperFINAL.pdf (29 June 2006).

Low, J. and Siesfeld, T. (1998) 'Wall Street Considers More than You Think', *Strategy and Leadership*, Vol. 26, No. 2: 24–30.

Mahoney, J. T. and Pandian, J. R. (1992) 'The Resource-Based View within the Conversation of Strategic Management', *Strategic Management Journal*, Vol. 13, No. 5: 363–80.

Manager-Magazin.de (2008) Milliardenverlust und Stellenabbau, www. manager-magazin.de/geld/artikel/0,2828,551614,00.html (17 July 2008).

McVey, H., Saini, P., McNellis, D. and Lim, F. (2005) US Portfolio Strategy: A Family Portrait, www.kennesaw.edu/fec/A%20Family%20Portrait%20Note%20081205.pdf (24 January 2008).

Mitchell, R. K., Agle, B. R. and Wood, D. J. (1997) 'Toward a Theory of Stakeholder Identification and Salience: Defining the Principle of Who and What Really Counts', *Academy of Management Review*, Vol. 22, No. 4: 853–86.

Nestlé (2005) Bericht zur Corporate Governance 2004, www.nestle.com/NR/rdonlyres/2FD785C8-5AC6-443D-816C-5EADA1746D3D/0/Governance ReportDE.pdf (1 November 2006).

Nike (2007) Innovate for a Better World, www.nike.com/nikebiz/nikeresponsibility/;bsessionid=FQ2GR202MUAECCQFTC2CF5AKAWMLSIZB# nikesapproach/main and www.nike.com/nikebiz/nikebiz.jhtml?page=25& cat=activefactories (1 November 2007).

Nonaka, I. and Takeuchi, H. (1995) *The Knowledge-Creating Company: How Japanese Companies Create the Dynamics of Innovation*, Oxford: Oxford University Press.

NZZ (2006) Bitterer Kaffee für die Starbucks-Anleger. Zu magere Umsatzzahlen drücken den Börsenkurs, www.nzz.ch/2006/08/04/bm/articleECSTB.html (3 November 2006).

NZZ (2007) Ciba-Aktien nicht mehr in New York gehandelt, www.nzz.ch/2007/06/26/bm/newzzF3DZX89B-12.html (8 October 2007).

Oakley, J. L. (2004) Linking Organizational Characteristics to Employee Attitudes and Behavior – A Look at the Downstream Effects on Market Response & Financial Performance, www.performanceforum.org/PFM/research/pdf/employee_engagement_study.pdf (26 June 2006).

OECD (2002) Third Eurasian Corporate Governance Roundtable Shareholder Rights, Equitable Treatment and the Role of the State, www.oecd.org/dataoecd/42/11/2098719.ppt (9 October 2007).

Oekom Research (2003) Nachhaltige Investments belohnen den Anleger, www.oekomresearch.de/ag/german/pressemeldungen/pm_performance03.htm (14 January 2008).

Office of Public Sector Information (OPSI) (2002) The Directors' Remuneration Report Regulations 2002. Statutory Instrument 2002 No. 1986, www.opsi.gov.uk/si/si2002/20021986.htm (4 October 2007).

Porsche (2007) Auch im Jahr 2007 profitieren Mitarbeiter der Porsche AG von der positiven Geschäftsentwicklung. Mit 5.200 Euro Sonderzahlung am Erfolg beteiligt, www.porsche.com/germany/aboutporsche/pressreleases/archiv2007/quarter4/?pool=germany&id=2007-10-05 (11 January 2008).

Porter, M. E. (1985) *Competitive Advantage: Creating and Sustaining Superior Performance*, New York: The Free Press.

Porter, M. E. (1991) 'Towards a Dynamic Theory of Strategy', *Strategic Management Journal*, Vol. 12, (Special Issue Winter): 95–117.

Porter, M. E. (1996) 'What is Strategy?' *Harvard Business Review*, November–December 1996: 61–78.

Porter, M. E. (1998) *Competitive Strategy: Techniques for Analyzing Industries and Competitors*, New York: The Free Press.

Porter, M. E. (2008) 'The Five Competitive Forces that Shape Strategy', *Harvard Business Review*, January: 79–93.

Porter, M. E. and Teisberg, E. O. (2006) *Redefining Health Care. Creating Value-Based Competition on Results*, Boston, MA: Harvard Business School Press.

Prahalad, C. K. and Hamel, G. (1990) 'The Core Competence of the Corporation', *Harvard Business Review*, May–June 1990: 79–91.

Prahalad, C. K. and Ramaswamy, V. (2005) 'Co-creating Unique Value with Customers', *Strategy & Leadership*, Vol. 32, No. 3: 4–9.

Preston, L. E. and O'Bannon, D. P. (1997) 'The Corporate Social–Financial Performance Relationship: A Typology and Analysis', *Business & Society*, Vol. 36: 419–29.

Raths, D. (2006) 'Business Ethcis 100 Best Corporate Citizens 2006. The Seventh Annual List of the Best-Managed U.S. Firms', *Business Ethics*, Vol. 20, No. 1, www.business-ethics.com/BE100_2006 (1 November 2007).

Reich, R. B. (2007) *Supercapitalism: The Transformation of Business, Democracy, and Everyday Life*, New York: Alfred A. Knopf.

Reuters (2007) E.ON to Delist from New York Stock Exchange, www.reuters.com/article/marketsNews/idUSWEB667220070821 (8 October 2007).

Sachs, S. (2000) *Die Rolle der Unternehmung in ihrer Interaktion mit der Gesellschaft*, Bern: Haupt.

Schaeffer (2006) Schaeffer's S&P 500 Index Hot Stocks Features RadioShack, Ford Motor, General Motors, PMC-Sierra, and Starbucks, http://findarticles.com/p/articles/mi_m0EIN/is_2006_July_7/ai_n16520505 (2 November 2007).

Starbucks (2005) Social Responsibility Newsletter: NGO Spotlight, www.starbucks.com/csrnewsletter/csrNGO.asp (8 January 2008).

Stiglitz, J. E. (2006) *Making Globalization Work: The Next Steps to Global Justice*, New York: Norton.

Stout, L. A. (2007) Why We Should Stop Teaching Dodge vs. Ford, http://papers.ssrn.com/sol3/papers.cfm?abstract_id=1013744 (30 October 2007).

Sturgess, J., Conway, N., Liefooghe, A. and Guest, D. E. (2003) 'The Psychological Contract as a Framework for Understanding Career Management and Commitment', *Academy of Management Conference Paper*, Seattle.

Sturgess, J., Guest, D. E., Conway, N. and Davey, K. M. (2001) 'What Difference Does It Make? A Longitudinal Study of the Relationship between Career Management and Organizational Commitment in the Early Years at Work', *Academy of Management Proceedings*, Washington, DC.

Swisscom (2007) Swisscom hat die Dekotierung von der New Yorker Börse eingeleitet, www.swisscom.com/GHQ/content/Media/Medienmitteilungen/2007/20070808_02_Dekotierung.htm (8 October 2007).

Tages-Anzeiger (2005) Verwaltungsrat droht mit Rücktritt, *Tages-Anzeiger*, Zürich, 10 April 2005.

Teece, D. J., Pisano, G. and Shuen, A. (1997) 'Dynamic Capabilities and Strategic Management', *Strategic Management Journal*, Vol. 18, No. 7: 509–33.

Tomorrow's-Company (2007) Tomorrow's Global Company: Challenges and Choices, London, www.tomorrowscompany.com/publications.aspx

von Frenz, C. (2003) Chronik einer Rekord-Pleite, http://www.manager magazin.de/unternehmen/artikel/0,2828,178836,00.html (4 October 2007).

Waddock, S., White, A., Goyder, M., Nelson, J., Lacy, P. and Post, J. E. (2007) Corporations and the 21st Century: How Do Today's Companies Need to Change to Meet Tomorrow's Needs?, www.caseplace.org/references/references_show.htm?doc_id=522575 (24 January 2008).

Watzlawick, P. (1988) 'Die Geschichte mit dem Hammer', in Watzlawick, P. (ed), *Anleitung zum Unglücklich sein*, München: R. Piper & Co., pp. 37–46.

Willetts, P. (2004) The Growth in the Number of NGOs with ECOSOC Consultative Status, www.staff.city.ac.uk/p.willetts/NGOS/NGO-GRPH.DOC (28 June 2006).

Yahoo! (2006) SMS History, http://in.mobile.yahoo.com/smshistory.html (1 April 2006).

ZKB (2007) Nachhaltige Anlagen: Der Klimawandel heizt kräftig ein, Anlagen Aktuell: Finanzmärkte und Empfehlungen im Blickpunkt – No. 5, Zurich.

# Index

*Key*: **bold** = extended discussion; b = box; f = figure; n = note; t = table; a number in square brackets denotes an allusion.